365 DAYS OF BLACK HISTORY

2011 ENGAGEMENT CALENDAR

WITH IMAGES FROM THE

LIBRARY OF CONGRESS

Pomegranate

Catalog No. H232

Published by Pomegranate Communications, Inc.
Box 808022, Petaluma CA 94975

Available in the UK and mainland Europe from Pomegranate Europe Ltd.
Unit 1, Heathcote Business Centre, Hurlbutt Road, Warwick, Warwickshire CV34 6TD, UK

Images courtesy of the Library of Congress, unless otherwise indicated. All rights reserved.
Text © 2010 IOKTS Productions • www.iokts.com

Pomegranate also publishes the wall calendars *A Journey into 365 Days of Black History, Romare Bearden,* and *African American Art,* and a wide variety of other calendars for 2011 in wall, mini wall, coloring, engagement, specialty, postcard, and 365-day tear-off formats. In addition to calendars, our extensive line of products and publications includes books, bookplates, notepads, coloring books, posters, postcards, notecards, invitations, thank you cards, magnets, mousepads, Knowledge Cards®, birthday books, journals, address books, jigsaw puzzles, designer gift wrap, gift enclosures, stationery sets, and bookmarks. For more information or to place an order, please contact Pomegranate Communications, Inc., 800 227 1428, www.pomegranate.com.

The Library of Congress, often called "the nation's memory," houses some 130 million items from around the world. Among these are the rich and varied collections of the Prints and Photographs Division, from which most of the photographs in this calendar are drawn. Duplicates of images appearing in this calendar that are accompanied by Library of Congress negative numbers (e.g., LC-USZ62-XXXX) may be ordered from the Library of Congress, Photoduplication Service, Washington, DC 20540-4570; telephone (202) 707-5640; fax (202) 707-1771.

Front cover:
Benin King and Two Attendants
Bronze relief
Photographer: John V. Twyman
Prints and Photographs Division, LC-USZC4-2141

Designed by Patrice Morris

Dates in color indicate US federal holidays.
Dates listed for all astronomical events in this calendar are based on Coordinated Universal Time (UTC), the worldwide system of civil timekeeping. UTC is essentially equivalent to Greenwich Mean Time.
Moon phases and American, Canadian, and UK holidays are noted.
Dates of Islamic holidays are based on promulgations of the Fiqh Council of North America.

● NEW MOON　　◐ FIRST QUARTER　　○ FULL MOON　　◑ LAST QUARTER

IOKTS PRODUCTIONS ("I Only Know the Story") is dedicated to the research of documented history for the purpose of exhibiting the contributions of black people from all cultures, races, and geographic locations. Through this work we strive to promote awareness, knowledge, and understanding among all people while furthering pride, dignity, and inspiration in those who identify directly with this heritage.

For more information, e-mail us at ioktspro@verizon.net or contact:

Mr. G. Theodore Catherine
IOKTS Productions
P.O. Box 11275
Takoma Park, MD 20913
(301) 270-1920

2011

JANUARY

s	m	t	w	t	f	s
						1
2	3	4	5	6	7	8
9	10	11	12	13	14	15
16	17	18	19	20	21	22
23	24	25	26	27	28	29
30	31					

FEBRUARY

s	m	t	w	t	f	s
		1	2	3	4	5
6	7	8	9	10	11	12
13	14	15	16	17	18	19
20	21	22	23	24	25	26
27	28					

MARCH

s	m	t	w	t	f	s
		1	2	3	4	5
6	7	8	9	10	11	12
13	14	15	16	17	18	19
20	21	22	23	24	25	26
27	28	29	30	31		

APRIL

s	m	t	w	t	f	s
					1	2
3	4	5	6	7	8	9
10	11	12	13	14	15	16
17	18	19	20	21	22	23
24	25	26	27	28	29	30

MAY

s	m	t	w	t	f	s
1	2	3	4	5	6	7
8	9	10	11	12	13	14
15	16	17	18	19	20	21
22	23	24	25	26	27	28
29	30	31				

JUNE

s	m	t	w	t	f	s
			1	2	3	4
5	6	7	8	9	10	11
12	13	14	15	16	17	18
19	20	21	22	23	24	25
26	27	28	29	30		

2011

JULY

s	m	t	w	t	f	s
					1	2
3	4	5	6	7	8	9
10	11	12	13	14	15	16
17	18	19	20	21	22	23
24	25	26	27	28	29	30
31						

AUGUST

s	m	t	w	t	f	s
	1	2	3	4	5	6
7	8	9	10	11	12	13
14	15	16	17	18	19	20
21	22	23	24	25	26	27
28	29	30	31			

SEPTEMBER

s	m	t	w	t	f	s
				1	2	3
4	5	6	7	8	9	10
11	12	13	14	15	16	17
18	19	20	21	22	23	24
25	26	27	28	29	30	

OCTOBER

s	m	t	w	t	f	s
						1
2	3	4	5	6	7	8
9	10	11	12	13	14	15
16	17	18	19	20	21	22
23	24	25	26	27	28	29
30	31					

NOVEMBER

s	m	t	w	t	f	s
		1	2	3	4	5
6	7	8	9	10	11	12
13	14	15	16	17	18	19
20	21	22	23	24	25	26
27	28	29	30			

DECEMBER

s	m	t	w	t	f	s
				1	2	3
4	5	6	7	8	9	10
11	12	13	14	15	16	17
18	19	20	21	22	23	24
25	26	27	28	29	30	31

Madame Lillian Evanti (American, 1890–1967)
Opera singer, activist

Anne Lillian Evans Tibbs was born in Washington, DC, to physician and educator Bruce Evans and educator Anne Brooks. As a lyric soprano, she became the first African American to sing with a professional European operatic company.

Born into an accomplished family that stressed the importance of education, Lillian graduated from Armstrong (Duke Ellington's alma mater), one of two public schools designated for black students in Washington, DC. Armstrong was founded by her father, who also served as principal.

After a short stint teaching, she enrolled at Howard University to pursue a career in music. To increase opportunities to perform in Europe, she blended her maiden name, Evans, with the surname of her husband, Roy Tibbs, to create an Italian-sounding stage name, Evanti. But the achievement of her dream of performing in Europe was counterbalanced by discrimination she experienced there, so she returned to the United States to continue her career.

Speaking and singing in five languages, Evanti set a high standard as a pioneering diva. She also cofounded the National Negro Opera Company to provide opportunities for blacks and was a popular performer with the company. Her trailblazing success inspired many African American women to pursue careers in opera. While winding down her career, she became a strong advocate and activist for D.C. Statehood, an ongoing movement to grant statehood to the District of Columbia.

Lillian Evanti
Photographer unknown
Prints and Photographs Division
LC-USZ62-107767

Dec • Jan

BANK HOLIDAY (UK)
Kujichagulia (Self-Determination). *To define ourselves, name ourselves, create for ourselves, and speak for ourselves.*

monday
27

BANK HOLIDAY (UK)
Ujima (Collective Work and Responsibility). *To build and maintain our community together; to make our sisters' and brothers' problems our problems and to solve them together.*

tuesday
28

Ujamaa (Cooperative Economics). *To build our own businesses, control the economics of our own communities, and share in all our communities' work and wealth.*

wednesday
29

Nia (Purpose). *To make our collective vocation the building and development of our community; to restore our people to their traditional greatness.*

thursday
30

NEW YEAR'S DAY HOLIDAY
Kuumba (Creativity). *To do as much as we can, in whatever way we can, to leave our community more beautiful and beneficial than it was when we inherited it.*

friday
31

NEW YEAR'S DAY
Kwanzaa ends: Imani (Faith). *To believe with all our hearts in our people, our parents, our teachers, our leaders, and the righteousness and victory of our struggle.*

1804: Haiti declares its independence.

1937: Lou Stovall, artist and master printmaker, is born in Athens, GA.

saturday
1

JANUARY

s	m	t	w	t	f	s
						1
2	3	4	5	6	7	8
9	10	11	12	13	14	15
16	17	18	19	20	21	22
23	24	25	26	27	28	29
30	31					

1898: Sadie Tanner Mossell Alexander, first African American to earn a PhD in economics, is born in Philadelphia.

1915: John Hope Franklin, historian, educator, and author of *From Slavery to Freedom: A History of Negro Americans*, is born in Rentiesville, OK.

sunday
2

Leopold Senghor (Senegalese, 1906–2001)
Politician
Leopold Senghor grew up in a rural African community outside Dakar, the capital of Senegal. One of twenty children, he rose from a small-town environment to become president of his country and a major influence in the movement for African liberation.

Senghor initially planned to become a priest, but upon earning a scholarship to study in Paris, he opted to complete his education at the Lycée Louis-le-Grand, an elite prep school. While in Paris, he learned of the Harlem Renaissance in America and drew inspiration from reading the works of its poets. Remaining in France after graduating, he became a French citizen, served in the military, and joined the French troops in WWII, during which he was captured by German soldiers. In a prison camp for 18 months, Senghor honed his writing skills and learned to speak German.

During the turbulent and transformational 1960s, blacks in America and Africa vigilantly challenged racism and injustice. In 1960 Senghor was elected president of Senegal, elevating his political status and giving his philosophical writings on African liberation international exposure. He coined the term "negritude" to describe Africans' pride in their culture.

Leopold Senghor's political philosophy is expressed in his writings, which have been translated into several languages. He has often stated, "All change, all production and generation are effected through the word."

Leopold Senghor
Photographer unknown
Prints and Photographs Division
LC-USZ62-119965

JANUARY

BANK HOLIDAY (CANADA, UK) — *monday*

1621: William Tucker is the first known child of Africans to be born in America.

1956: Colored Methodist Church, established in 1870, officially changes its name to Christian Methodist Episcopal Church.

3

BANK HOLIDAY (SCOTLAND) — *tuesday*

1787: Prince Hall, founder of the first black Masonic lodge, and others petition the Massachusetts legislature for funds to return to Africa, the first recorded effort by blacks to do so.

1920: Andrew "Rube" Foster organizes the first black baseball league, the Negro National League.

4

---

wednesday

1911: Kappa Alpha Psi fraternity is chartered as a national organization.

1931: Alvin Ailey, dancer and founder of his eponymous company, is born in Rogers, TX.

5

---

thursday

1993: Jazz trumpeter John Birks "Dizzy" Gillespie dies in Englewood, NJ.

1996: Recycling Black Dollars, an organization of black businesses, campaigns for "Change Bank Day" to benefit black-owned financial institutions.

6

---

friday

1891: Folklorist and novelist Zora Neale Hurston is born in Notasulga, AL.

1997: Former South African president Pieter W. Botha is prosecuted for refusing to appear before the nation's truth commission.

7

---

saturday

1922: Col. Charles Young, first African American to achieve that rank in the US Army, dies in Lagos, Nigeria.

8

JANUARY

s	m	t	w	t	f	s
						1
2	3	4	5	6	7	8
9	10	11	12	13	14	15
16	17	18	19	20	21	22
23	24	25	26	27	28	29
30	31					

sunday

1866: Fisk University is founded in Nashville.

1906: Renowned poet and writer Paul Laurence Dunbar dies in Dayton, OH.

1914: Phi Beta Sigma fraternity is founded at Howard University.

9

Dr. Eric Williams (Trinidadian, 1911–1981)
Prime minister, Trinidad and Tobago
Known as the "father of the nation" of Trinidad and Tobago, Eric Williams became prime minister of the two-island republic in 1961, when it was still under British colonial rule, and held that office until his death. Williams led the country into the West Indies Federation and ultimately to independence.

Born in Trinidad, Williams graduated with honors from Queen's Royal College in Port of Spain and attended Oxford University on a scholarship, earning his PhD degree in 1938. In his doctoral dissertation, Williams argued that Great Britain had freed the West Indian slaves more for economic than for humanitarian reasons. American historian Henry Steele Commager described the dissertation as "one of the most learned, most penetrating, and most significant works that has appeared in the field of history." Based on his dissertation, Williams's 1944 book, *Capitalism and Slavery*, was lauded as a groundbreaking examination of the role of the African slave trade in Europe's industrial revolution. His autobiography, *Inward Hunger: The Education of a Prime Minister*, was published in 1969.

Today, Williams's legacy continues through the work of his daughter, Erica Williams Connell, who has established an Eric Williams foundation and museum in Miami, Florida.

Dr. Eric Williams
Photographer unknown
Prints and Photographs Division
LC-USZ62-125505

JANUARY

1864: George Washington Carver, scientist and inventor, is born in Diamond Grove, MO.

1924: Drummer Max Roach, influential in the development of modern jazz, is born in New Land, NC.

monday

10

1940: Benjamin O. Davis Sr. becomes the US Army's first black general.

tuesday

11

1890: Mordecai W. Johnson, first black president of Howard University (a position he will hold for 34 years), is born in Paris, TN. He goes on to receive the NAACP's Spingarn Medal in 1929.

1996: Pioneering sports journalist Sam Skinner dies in Burlingame, CA.

2010: A 7.0 magnitude earthquake devastates the island nation of Haiti.

wednesday

12

1913: Delta Sigma Theta sorority is founded at Howard University.

thursday

13

1916: Author John Oliver Killens is born in Macon, GA.

1940: Julian Bond, civil rights leader and Georgia state senator, is born in Nashville.

friday

14

1908: Alpha Kappa Alpha sorority is founded at Howard University by Ethel Hedgeman Lyle.

saturday

15

JANUARY

s	m	t	w	t	f	s
						1
2	3	4	5	6	7	8
9	10	11	12	13	14	15
16	17	18	19	20	21	22
23	24	25	26	27	28	29
30	31					

1920: Zeta Phi Beta sorority is founded at Howard University.

1974: Noted singer-composer Leon Bukasa of Zaire dies.

sunday

16

Katherine Dunham (American, 1909–2006)
Anthropologist, dancer, choreographer
Through Ballet Negre and the school that bore her name, Katherine Dunham played a leading role in the development of ballet and African dance in the United States. Her achievement, comparable to that of Twyla Tharp, Merce Cunningham, or Martha Graham, bears a distinctively anthropological touch: before founding her company she wrote a number of scholarly books and articles on Afro-Caribbean dance based on field work in Haiti and Jamaica.

Born in Joliet, Illinois, Dunham used her degree in anthropology to analyze dance in Brazilian and Caribbean cultures. She was particularly fond of Haiti, where she purchased a home and actively supported campaigns for Haitian rights. At the age of 82 Dunham went on a 47-day hunger strike protesting the deportation of over 10,000 Haitian refugees who had fled Haiti and landed on American shores.

As an award-winning dance pioneer, Dunham was unique in her application of anthropology to understand dance in various cultures. Choreographers continue to employ the "Dunham technique."

Katherine Dunham in *Tropical Revue,* at the Martin Beck Theatre, 1943
Photographer: Alfredo Valente
Prints and Photographs Division
LC-DIG-ppmsca-05801

JANUARY

MARTIN LUTHER KING JR. DAY

1882: Lewis H. Latimer is granted a patent for the process of manufacturing carbon filaments for lightbulbs.

1942: Muhammad Ali, heavyweight boxing champion, is born in Louisville, KY.

monday

17

1856: Daniel Hale Williams, first physician to perform open-heart surgery and founder of Provident Hospital in Chicago, is born in Hollidaysburg, PA.

tuesday

18

1887: Clementine Hunter, noted African American painter, is born in Natchitoches, LA.

1918: John H. Johnson, editor and publisher of *Ebony* and *Jet* magazines, is born in Arkansas City, AR.

wednesday

○ 19

1974: Stevie Wonder plays a gig at Rainbow Theatre, London, after recovering from a car accident five months earlier that almost killed him.

2009: Barack Obama, inaugurated as the 44th president of the United States, becomes the country's first African American president.

thursday

20

1993: Congressman Mike Espy of Mississippi is confirmed as secretary of agriculture.

friday

21

1906: Pioneering aviator Willa Brown-Chappell is born in Glasgow, KY.

1935: Singer Sam Cooke, best known for "You Send Me" and "Twisting the Night Away," is born in Chicago.

saturday

22

JANUARY

s	m	t	w	t	f	s
						1
2	3	4	5	6	7	8
9	10	11	12	13	14	15
16	17	18	19	20	21	22
23	24	25	26	27	28	29
30	31					

1941: Richard Wright is awarded the NAACP's Spingarn Medal.

1964: The 24th Amendment is ratified, abolishing the poll tax.

sunday

23

Patrice Lumumba (Congolese, 1925–1961)
First prime minister of the Republic of the Congo
Patrice Lumumba led the Belgian Congo to independence in 1960 and was duly elected prime minister of the newly formed Republic of the Congo (later renamed the Democratic Republic of the Congo). Lumumba was a dynamic leader who stressed independence from colonial rule and solidarity among African nations. "What we want for our country," he said, "is its right to an honorable life, to a dignity without stain and to an independence without restriction." His term in office, however, was cut short—within months he was overthrown, imprisoned, and assassinated under circumstances that remain unclear. Lumumba's resistance to colonial rule had met with opposition from Belgium, which had prospered greatly from unimpeded access to the Congo's rich resources, and there were rumors of US government interest in removing Lumumba from office to avert a feared spread of Communism.

Today the Democratic Republic of the Congo remains impoverished as businesses reap huge profits from its mineral resources—gold, coltan, tin, and tungsten, used in computers, cell phones, and other electronic devices.

Patrice Lumumba speaking with supporters in his effort to regain office, Léopoldville, Congo, 1960
Photographer unknown
Prints and Photographs Division
LC-USZ62-130458

JANUARY

1985: Tom Bradley, four-term mayor of Los Angeles, receives the NAACP's Spingarn Medal for public service.

monday

24

1890: The National Afro-American League, a pioneering black protest organization, is founded in Chicago.

1966: Constance Baker Motley becomes the first African American woman to be appointed to a federal judgeship.

tuesday

25

1927: Singer, dancer, and actor Eartha Mae Kitt is born in Columbia, SC.

1944: Angela Yvonne Davis, political activist and educator, is born in Birmingham, AL.

wednesday

26

1972: Gospel music legend Mahalia Jackson dies in Evergreen Park, IL.

thursday

27

1944: Matthew Henson receives a joint medal from Congress as codiscoverer of the North Pole.

friday

28

1872: Francis L. Cardoza is elected South Carolina state treasurer.

1926: Violette Neatley Anderson becomes the first African American woman admitted to practice before the US Supreme Court.

saturday

29

JANUARY

s	m	t	w	t	f	s
						1
2	3	4	5	6	7	8
9	10	11	12	13	14	15
16	17	18	19	20	21	22
23	24	25	26	27	28	29
30	31					

1844: Richard Theodore Greener becomes the first African American to graduate from Harvard University.

sunday

30

Chinua Achebe (Nigerian, b. 1930)
Author

Chinua Achebe is one of Africa's most celebrated authors. His first novel, *Things Fall Apart* (1958), is the most widely read novel in African literature; it has been published in fifty different languages and has sold more than 2 million copies. Addressing the adverse effects of European colonialism on traditional African societies, such as that of the Igbo, it is required reading throughout the continent and serves as a model of African literature.

Achebe's academic excellence earned him a scholarship to complete his college education. Seeking opportunity, he moved to Nigeria's capital city, Lagos, and began writing of his experiences. He wrote several novels, gaining worldwide popularity, before actively supporting the secession of Biafra, a southeastern region of Nigeria. This conflict would bring war, famine, and suffering for Achebe and the Igbo people.

In a controversial lecture, Achebe criticized Joseph Conrad and his classic work *Heart of Darkness*. Achebe said, "Conrad was a seductive writer. He could pull his reader into the fray. And if it were not for what he said about me and my people, I would probably be thinking only of that seduction."

Chinua Achebe
Photographer: Lili Iravani
Public Affairs Office
Image of Chinua Achebe used with permission of The Wylie Agency LLC.

JAN • FEB

1919: Jackie Robinson, first African American to play in major league baseball, is born in Cairo, GA. 2006: Coretta Scott King dies in Mexico. 2009: In Molo, Kenya, at least 113 people are killed and over 200 injured when an oil spill is ignited.	*monday* 31 ₃₁
1865: John S. Rock becomes the first black attorney to practice before the US Supreme Court. 1902: Prolific poet Langston Hughes is born in Joplin, MO.	*tuesday* 1 ₃₂
1915: Biologist Ernest E. Just receives the Spingarn Medal for his pioneering research in fertilization and cell division.	*wednesday* 2 ₃₃
LUNAR NEW YEAR 1947: Percival Prattis, of *Our World in New York City*, becomes the first black news correspondent admitted to the House and Senate press galleries in Washington, DC. 1948: Portraitist and illustrator Laura Wheeler Waring dies in Philadelphia.	*thursday* ● 3 ₃₄
1913: Rosa Parks, initiator of the Montgomery, AL, bus boycott, is born in Tuskegee, AL. 1969: The Popular Liberation Movement of Angola begins armed struggle against the country's colonial Portuguese government.	*friday* 4 ₃₅
1934: Hank Aaron, a major league baseball home run king, is born in Mobile, AL. 1994: White supremacist Byron de la Beckwith is convicted of the murder of Medgar Evers, more than 30 years after Evers was ambushed and shot in the back.	*saturday* 5 ₃₆

FEBRUARY

s	m	t	w	t	f	s
			1	2	3	4	5
6	7	8	9	10	11	12
13	14	15	16	17	18	19
20	21	22	23	24	25	26
27	28

1926: Negro History Week, originated by Carter G. Woodson, is observed for the first time.

1993: Arthur Ashe, tennis player, humanitarian, and activist, dies in New York City.

sunday

6
₃₇

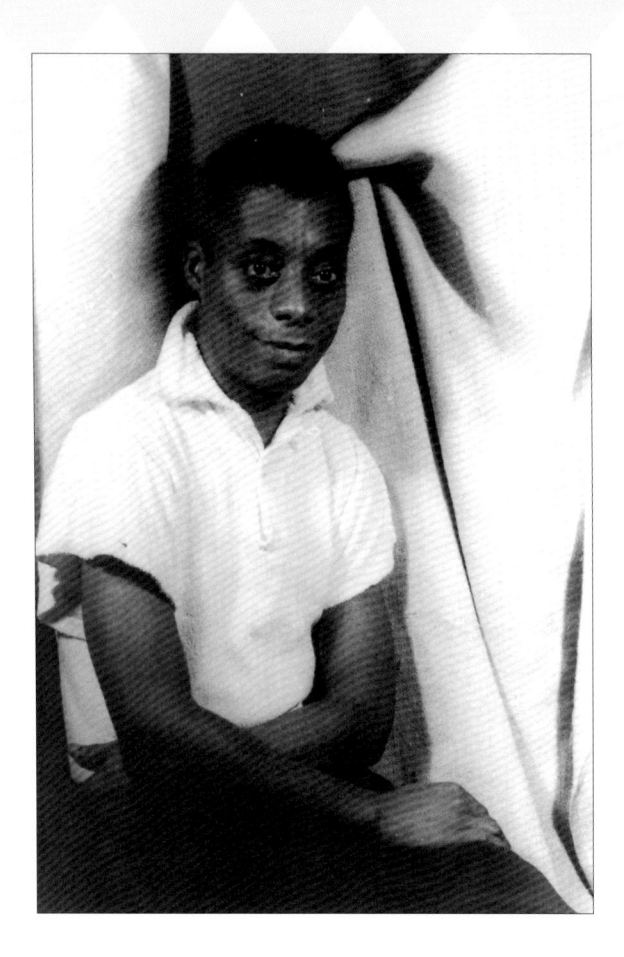

James Baldwin (American, 1924–1987)
Novelist
James Baldwin was one of the most influential American writers of the turbulent 1960s. His fiery passion and progressive ideas reflected the times, yet his views on racism, sexism, and society ignited debates.

Born into a large and poor family in Harlem, Baldwin attended the prestigious DeWitt Clinton High School in the Bronx, whose alumni include Richard Avedon, Romare Bearden, basketball great "Tiny" Nate Archibald, and many other notables. Drawn to the lively community of artists and writers, he moved to Greenwich Village, a place that permitted him to discover his talent and his sexuality without putting him down.

In 1948, like many African Americans who sought refuge from racism, Baldwin became an expatriate in Paris, France, where he spent most of his life. He kept company with Richard Wright, Langston Hughes, and Lorraine Hansberry, and he was a major influence on the singer Nina Simone.

Baldwin's eloquent reflections on being a gay black man in America were controversial, but he was broadly respected as an intelligent, progressive writer who never ceased to demand equality. His novels, *Go Tell It on the Mountain* (1953), *Giovanni's Room* (1956), *Another Country* (1962), *Tell Me How Long the Train's Been Gone* (1968), *If Beale Street Could Talk* (1974), and *Just Above My Head* (1979), are still studied and widely read.

James Baldwin, 1955
Photographer: Carl Van Vechten
Prints and Photographs Division
LC-USZ62-42481

FEBRUARY

Independence Day (Grenada) — *monday* **7** 38

1925: Marcus Garvey enters federal prison in Atlanta, GA.
1944: Harry S. McAlphin of Atlanta's *Daily World* becomes the first black journalist accredited to attend White House press conferences. — *tuesday* **8** 39

1944: Alice Walker, Pulitzer Prize–winning author, is born in Eatonton, GA. — *wednesday* **9** 40

1780: Capt. Paul Cuffee and six other black residents of Massachusetts petition the state legislature for the right to vote.
1869: Nat Love, former slave from Tennessee, goes west to make his fortune. He will become known as Deadwood Dick, one of the most famous cowboys, black or white, in history. — *thursday* **10** 41

1990: Nelson Mandela is released from a South African prison after 27 years as a political prisoner.
2008: Morgan Tsvangirai is sworn in as prime minister of Zimbabwe following a power-sharing deal with President Robert Mugabe. — *friday* ◐ **11** 42

1896: Isaac Burns Murphy, one of the greatest jockeys of all time, dies in Lexington, KY. — *saturday* **12** 43

FEBRUARY

s	m	t	w	t	f	s
		1	2	3	4	5
6	7	8	9	10	11	12
13	14	15	16	17	18	19
20	21	22	23	24	25	26
27	28					

1907: Wendell P. Dabney establishes *The Union*, a Cincinnati paper whose motto is "For no people can become great without being united, for in union, there is strength."
1970: Joseph L. Searles becomes the first black member of the New York Stock Exchange. — *sunday* **13** 44

Saint Maurice
Egyptian, third century
More than seventy towns have been named in honor of Saint Maurice; five cathedrals and innumerable churches have been consecrated in his name. His sacred relic, the Sword of Saint Maurice, was last used in 1916 in the coronation of Emperor Charles of Austria as king of Hungary.

Maurice was captain of the Theban Legion, a unit in the Roman army that had been recruited from Egypt and consisted of 6,600 Christian soldiers. He and other members of the Theban Legion were martyred for their refusal to follow the orders of the Roman emperor Maximian Herculius to persecute other Christians for rebellion.

Saint Maurice and his Theban Legion are celebrated on September 22 each year.

Saint Maurice
Painting by Matthias Grünewald
General Collections

FEBRUARY

VALENTINE'S DAY

1817: Frederick Douglass, "the Great Emancipator," is born in Talbot County, MD.

1867: Morehouse College is founded in Augusta, GA; it later moves to Atlanta.

monday

14 45

1961: US activists and African nationalists disrupt UN sessions to protest the slaying of Congo premier Patrice Lumumba.

tuesday

15 46

1826: *The Liberia Herald*, first newspaper printed in Africa, is published by C. L. Force of Boston.

1923: Bessie Smith makes her first recording, "Down-Hearted Blues," which sells 800,000 copies for Columbia Records.

wednesday

16 47

1938: Mary Frances Berry, first woman to serve as chancellor of a major research university (University of Colorado), is born in Nashville.

1982: Pianist Thelonious Monk, a founding father of modern jazz, dies from a massive stroke in Weehawken, NJ.

thursday

17 48

National Independence Day (Gambia)

1688: Quakers at Germantown, PA, adopt the first formal antislavery resolution in American history.

friday

○ **18** 49

1919: W. E. B. Du Bois organizes the second Pan-African Congress in Paris.

saturday

19 50

FEBRUARY

s	m	t	w	t	f	s
		1	2	3	4	5
6	7	8	9	10	11	12
13	14	15	16	17	18	19
20	21	22	23	24	25	26
27	28					

1927: Sidney Poitier, first African American to win an Academy Award in a starring role, is born in Miami.

1929: Wallace Thurman's play *Harlem* begins a successful run on Broadway.

sunday

20 51

Pelé (Brazilian, b. 1940)
Soccer player
Pelé—born Edison (Edson) Arantes do Nascimento in Três Corações, Minas Gerais, Brazil—is indisputably the greatest soccer player in history. Possessing lightning speed, nimble feet, and an uncanny ability to elude defenders, Pelé consistently scored goals and soared to superstardom and worldwide recognition.

The soccer legend says he is a "chip off the old block," crediting his father, Dondinho—himself a soccer player, whose career was short-lived—for his ability. From the start Pelé performed magnificently at every level of league play, including four trips to the World Cup with the Brazilian national team. Pelé was declared a national treasure by the government of Brazil.

As soccer gained popularity in the United States, Pelé became an ambassador for the sport, signing a lucrative contract with the newly formed North American Soccer League. As a professional he was magnificent; his play helped make soccer an American sport.

Pelé
Photographer unknown
Prints and Photographs Division
LC-USZ62-120850

FEBRUARY

PRESIDENTS' DAY

1965: El-Hajj Malik el-Shabazz (Malcolm X), American black nationalist, is assassinated in New York City.

monday

21

1841: Grafton Tyler Brown, one of California's first African American painters, is born in Harrisburg, PA.

1962: Wilt Chamberlain sets an NBA record with 34 attempted free throws.

tuesday

22

Republic Day (Guyana)

1972: Political activist Angela Davis is released from jail.

wednesday

23

1966: Military leaders oust Kwame Nkrumah, president of Ghana, while he is in Beijing on a peace mission to stop the Vietnam War.

2008: Raúl Castro is elected president of Cuba after his brother Fidel resigns.

thursday

◐ 24

1978: Daniel "Chappie" James, first African American four-star general, dies in Colorado Springs, CO.

1991: Adrienne Mitchell becomes the first black woman in the US armed forces to die in combat. She is killed in her military barracks in Saudi Arabia during the Persian Gulf War.

friday

25

1926: Theodore "Tiger" Flowers (aka "the Georgia Deacon") defeats Harry Greb in New York City, becoming the first black middleweight champion of the world.

1928: Singer Antoine "Fats" Domino is born in New Orleans.

saturday

26

FEBRUARY

s	m	t	w	t	f	s
		1	2	3	4	5
6	7	8	9	10	11	12
13	14	15	16	17	18	19
20	21	22	23	24	25	26
27	28					

Independence Day (Dominican Republic)

1872: Charlotte Ray graduates from Howard University's law school, becoming the first female African American lawyer.

sunday

27

Elizabeth Keckley (American, 1818–1907)
Slave, dressmaker, abolitionist, White House memoirist
Elizabeth Keckley, affectionately called Lizzie, was born in Virginia to slaves George and Agnes Hobbs. While in her teens Lizzie was sold to another slave owner. A forced relationship with a white friend of her new owner left her with a child, George, named after her father.

Lizzie was later married briefly, after which she focused on obtaining freedom for herself and young George. She eventually paid off her owner, moved to Baltimore, and established a school for young black women, where she taught sewing and the art of being a lady. Word of her sewing talents quickly spread, and she soon became the seamstress for wives of Washington politicians—most notably Mary Todd Lincoln, the wife of President Abraham Lincoln. Keckley's elegant dresses helped Mrs. Lincoln shed her image of a backwoods, unsophisticated first lady.

Elizabeth Keckley related her life experiences in the book *Behind the Scenes: Thirty Years a Slave, and Four Years in the White House.*

Elizabeth Keckley
Photograph courtesy Smithsonian Institution

FEB • MAR

1948: Sgt. Cornelius F. Adjetey becomes the first martyr for the national independence of Ghana.

monday

28

1871: James Milton Turner is named minister to Liberia, becoming the first black American diplomat accredited to an African country.

1914: Ralph Waldo Ellison, author of the award-winning *Invisible Man*, is born in Oklahoma City.

tuesday

1

1955: Claudette Colvin refuses to give up her seat on a bus in Montgomery, AL, nine months before Rosa Parks's arrest for the same action sparks the Montgomery bus boycott.

wednesday

2

Martyr's Day (Malawi)

1821: Thomas L. Jennings is the first African American to be granted a US patent, for his technique to "dry-scour" clothes.

thursday

3

1932: Zensi Miriam Makeba, "Empress of African Song," is born in Prospect Township, South Africa.

friday

● 4

1770: Crispus Attucks is killed in the Boston Massacre, marking the start of the American Revolution.

saturday

5

MARCH

s	m	t	w	t	f	s
		1	2	3	4	5
6	7	8	9	10	11	12
13	14	15	16	17	18	19
20	21	22	23	24	25	26
27	28	29	30	31		

Independence Day (Ghana)

1857: US Supreme Court rules against citizenship for African Americans in the Dred Scott decision.

sunday

6

Mal Whitfield (American, b. 1924)
Olympic athlete, WWII Tuskegee Airman
"Marvelous" Mal Whitfield has influenced the worlds of sports and diplomacy through his accomplishments as an Olympic track and field champion and by his work as a sports goodwill ambassador with the US Department of State. He earned three Olympic gold medals in track and field, won the James E. Sullivan Memorial Award for top amateur athlete in the United States, and was elected to the US Olympics Hall of Fame.

As a young man, Whitfield was inspired by Olympic athletes Eddie Tolan and Jesse Owens, diligently honing his running skills while attending Ohio State University, Jesse Owens's alma mater. Whitfield dominated the 800-meter race between 1946 and 1955, winning two consecutive Olympic gold medals in London (1948) and in Helsinki (1952).

During his 34 years of diplomatic service he traveled to more than 100 countries, conducting training clinics and also counseling and coaching such noted runners as Mamo Wolde and Meruts Yifter of Ethiopia and Kip Keino of Kenya. The fact that African runners have dominated major marathons in the US is partly due to the pioneer efforts of Marvelous Mal Whitfield.

Mal Whitfield
Photographer: Douglas Jones
Prints and Photographs Division

MARCH

1539: Estevanico (or Esteban) de Dorantes, a native of Azamoro, Morocco, sets out to explore what is now the southwestern United States.

monday

7

MARDI GRAS
INTERNATIONAL WOMEN'S DAY

1876: After three years of controversy, the US Senate refuses to seat P. B. S. Pinchback, elected as a Louisiana senator in 1873.

1977: Henry L. Marsh III is elected first black mayor of Richmond, VA.

tuesday

8

ASH WEDNESDAY

1914: The "new" Southern University campus opens in Scotlandville, LA, with 9 teachers and 47 students.

1919: Nora Douglas Holt and other black Chicago musicians form the Chicago Musical Association.

wednesday

9

1845: Women's rights activist Hallie Quinn Brown is born in Pittsburgh, PA.

1963: Actor Jasmine Guy, known as Whitley in the TV series *A Different World*, is born in Boston.

thursday

10

1948: Dr. Reginald Weir of New York City wins his first match in the USLTA Tennis Championship Tournament.

friday

11

1791: Benjamin Banneker and Pierre Charles L'Enfant are commissioned to plan and develop Washington, DC.

saturday

◐ **12**

MARCH

s	m	t	w	t	f	s
		1	2	3	4	5
6	7	8	9	10	11	12
13	14	15	16	17	18	19
20	21	22	23	24	25	26
27	28	29	30	31		

DAYLIGHT SAVING TIME BEGINS

1773: Jean-Baptiste Pointe du Sable founds the city of Chicago.

1943: Frank Dixon becomes the first great black miler in track, winning the Columbian Mile in New York City in a record time of 4 minutes, 9.6 seconds.

sunday

13

Martina Arroyo (American, b. 1937)
Opera singer
An operatic performer in a long line of African American divas—from Sissieretta Jones, called "the Black Patti" after the Italian opera singer Adelina Patti, to Marian Anderson and Leontyne Price—Martina Arroyo has always been uniquely self-motivated, hardworking, and eager to share her gifts. Her father, Demetrio Arroyo, was an engineer born in Puerto Rico; her mother, Lucille Washington, was an African American from Charleston, South Carolina. As a teenager, Arroyo exhibited exceptional singing talent and a disciplined, well-planned approach to achieving success.

After her debut at New York's Metropolitan Opera in 1959, Arroyo rose to become a world-renowned spinto soprano. She performed at the Paris Opera, Milan's La Scala, London's Covent Garden, the Vienna State Opera, and the Buenos Aires Teatro Colón. She was a guest on the *Tonight Show Starring Johnny Carson* more than twenty times, and she is a frequent guest and moderator on the Met's radio broadcast *Singers' Roundtable*.

Arroyo retired from singing in 1989 but has been very active as a teacher. In 2003 she established the Martina Arroyo Foundation to aid young artists pursuing professional careers in opera.

Martina Arroyo as Aida, 1961
Photographer unknown
Prints and Photographs Division
LC-USZ62-138719

MARCH

1933: Composer, musician, and producer Quincy Delight Jones is born in Chicago.

monday

14

1947: John Lee becomes the first African American commissioned officer in the US Navy.

1968: *Life* magazine calls Jimi Hendrix "the most spectacular guitarist in the world."

tuesday

15

1827: John Russwurm, first African American college graduate, begins publication of *Freedom's Journal* with Samuel Cornish.

1995: Mississippi ratifies the 13th Amendment, which abolishes slavery, 130 years after all but three other states had approved it.

wednesday

16

ST. PATRICK'S DAY

1865: Aaron Anderson wins the navy's Medal of Honor for his heroic actions aboard USS *Wyandank* during the Civil War.

1867: Educator Ida Rebecca Cummings is born in Baltimore.

thursday

17

1901: Renowned painter William H. Johnson is born in Florence, SC.

1992: Singer Donna Summer gets a star on Hollywood's Walk of Fame.

friday

18

PURIM (BEGINS AT SUNSET)

1930: Jazz saxophonist Ornette Coleman is born in Fort Worth, TX.

1939: Langston Hughes founds the New Negro Theater in Los Angeles. Its first performance is his play *Don't You Want to Be Free?*

saturday

○ **19**

MARCH

s	m	t	w	t	f	s
		1	2	3	4	5
6	7	8	9	10	11	12
13	14	15	16	17	18	19
20	21	22	23	24	25	26
27	28	29	30	31		

VERNAL EQUINOX 23:21 UTC

1883: Jan Matzeliger receives a patent for the shoe-lasting machine, which launches mass production of shoes.

sunday

20

Africa

This striking image is from the collection of Gary Yanker, who collected protest and propaganda posters, amassing thousands. In 1975 Yanker donated his collection to the Library of Congress. A persistent collector, he contacted hundreds of companies to request copies of their advertising posters. Many of the items from his collection can be seen in the book *Prop Art,* published in 1972 by Darien House.

This poster of Africa with a woman inside was created in 1971. The red, black, and green colors were strongly identified with the Black Power movement of the day. The figure suggests the leading role of women in Africa, from the birth of humankind to the rebirth of nations as they shook off the chains of colonialism.

Africa, c. 1971
Poster design: Zash MJB
Prints and Photographs Division
LC-USZC4-14417

# MARCH

1965: Martin Luther King Jr. leads thousands of marchers from Selma, heading for Montgomery, AL, to dramatize denial of voting rights to African Americans.

monday

21

1492: Alonzo Pietro, explorer, sets sail with Christopher Columbus.

tuesday

22

1985: Patricia Roberts Harris, Cabinet member and ambassador, dies in Washington, DC.

wednesday

23

1907: Nurse and aviator Janet Harmon Bragg is born in Griffin, GA.

thursday

24

1931: Ida B. Wells-Barnett, journalist, antilynching activist, and founding member of the NAACP, dies in Chicago.

1939: Toni Cade Bambara, noted fiction writer *(The Sea Birds Are Still Alive; Gorilla, My Love; The Salt Eaters),* is born in New York City.

friday

25

1886: Hugh N. Mulzac, the first black to captain an American merchant marine ship (SS *Booker T. Washington,* 1942), is born in the West Indies.

saturday

◐ 26

MARCH

s	m	t	w	t	f	s
		1	2	3	4	5
6	7	8	9	10	11	12
13	14	15	16	17	18	19
20	21	22	23	24	25	26
27	28	29	30	31		

SUMMER TIME BEGINS (UK)

1872: Musician Cleveland Luca, member of the famous Luca Family Quartet and composer of the Liberian national anthem, dies in Liberia.

1924: Jazz singer Sarah Vaughan, "the Divine One," is born in Newark, NJ.

sunday

27

George Augustus Polgreen Bridgetower (Polish, 1780–1860)
Composer, musician
George Augustus Bridgetower was a musical genius. Born in Biala, Poland, he came of age in an era of superb classical musicians and composers such as Beethoven. Bridgetower's father, John Frederick Bridgetower, is believed to have been a slave from the Caribbean, and his mother, Marie Ann, was of Eastern European ancestry.

The violin virtuoso made his debut performance as a soloist in Paris at the age of nine. Soon afterward, Bridgetower relocated to England, where the Prince of Wales (and future George IV) supported his musical education by placing him under the tutelage of acclaimed musical instructors.

Accompanied by composer Ludwig van Beethoven on piano, Bridgetower performed the premiere of Beethoven's *Sonata for Violin and Piano No. 9 in A Minor, Op. 47,* in Vienna in 1803, and the composer originally dedicated the work to Bridgetower. However, their relationship was strained by an event between Bridgetower and a female friend of Beethoven, prompting the composer to rededicate the sonata, which today is known as the Kreutzer Sonata.

Bridgetower was also a respected piano instructor, a member of the Professional Music Society, and an original member of the Royal Philharmonic Society, founded in 1813.

George Bridgetower
Drawing by Henry Edridge
Music Division

MAR • APR

1870: Jonathan S. Wright becomes the first African American state supreme court justice in South Carolina.	*monday* 28
1918: Singer and actor Pearl Bailey is born in Newport News, VA. 1945: Basketball guard Walt Frazier is born in Atlanta. The future Hall of Famer will lead the New York Knicks to NBA championships in 1970 and 1973.	*tuesday* 29
1948: Trailblazing fashion model Naomi Sims is born in Oxford, MS.	*wednesday* 30
1871: Jack Johnson, first African American heavyweight boxing champion, is born in Galveston, TX. 1988: Toni Morrison wins the Pulitzer Prize for her novel *Beloved*.	*thursday* 31
1930: Zauditu, first female monarch of Ethiopia, dies.	*friday* 1
1796: Haitian revolt leader Toussaint L'Ouverture commands French forces at Santo Domingo.	*saturday* 2

APRIL

s	m	t	w	t	f	s
					1	2
3	4	5	6	7	8	9
10	11	12	13	14	15	16
17	18	19	20	21	22	23
24	25	26	27	28	29	30

MOTHERING SUNDAY (UK) — *sunday* 3

1934: Richard Mayhew, revolutionary landscape artist, is born in Amityville, NY.

1984: John Thompson of Georgetown University becomes the first African American coach to win an NCAA basketball tournament.

Chester Himes (American, 1909–1984)
Author
Chester Himes was born in Jefferson City, Missouri, to parents who were both teachers. He was naturally gifted intellectually, but striving for career success while dealing with setbacks and racial animosity proved to be challenging. Himes outwardly expressed his growing anger, which resulted in trouble with the law. He was expelled from Ohio State University, and beginning in 1928 he served seven and a half years in the state penitentiary for armed robbery. Oddly, going to prison was Himes's salvation; that was where he began to write of his life experiences and express his anger creatively. Several of his books featuring black detectives became popular enough to be adapted for film, including *If He Hollers Let Him Go, Cotton Comes to Harlem,* and the latter's sequel, *Come Back, Charleston Blue.*

Himes emigrated to France, where he gained literary fame and kept company with friends such as the famous African American writers James Baldwin and Richard Wright. These fiery writers were of like mind and were an inspiration to Himes.

Chester Himes
Photographer: Carl Van Vechten
Prints and Photographs Division
LC-USZ62-105578

APRIL

Independence Day (Senegal)
1968: Martin Luther King Jr. is assassinated in Memphis.
2002: Angola's government and UNITA rebels sign a peace treaty ending that country's civil war.

monday
4

1937: Colin Powell, first African American to serve as chairman of the Joint Chiefs of Staff and US secretary of state, is born in New York City.

tuesday
5

1798: Noted scout James P. Beckwourth is born in Fredericksburg, VA. He discovered the pass in the Sierra Nevada that bears his name.
1905: W. Warrick Cardozo, physician and pioneering researcher in sickle cell anemia, is born in Washington, DC.

wednesday
6

1867: Johnson C. Smith University is founded in Charlotte, NC.
1915: Jazz and blues legend Billie Holiday is born in East Baltimore, MD.

thursday
7

1974: Hank Aaron breaks Babe Ruth's major league record with 715 career home runs.
1990: Percy Julian and George Washington Carver are the first black inventors admitted into the National Inventors Hall of Fame.

friday
8

National Day (Sierra Leone)
1898: Actor and singer Paul Robeson is born in Princeton, NJ.
1950: Juanita Hall is the first black to win a Tony Award, for her portrayal of Bloody Mary in *South Pacific*.

saturday
9

APRIL

s	m	t	w	t	f	s
					1	2
3	4	5	6	7	8	9
10	11	12	13	14	15	16
17	18	19	20	21	22	23
24	25	26	27	28	29	30

1943: Arthur Ashe, first African American to win the men's singles title at both the US Open and Wimbledon, is born in Richmond, VA.

sunday
10

Black Progress
This poster features the cover art from a book published by the Illinois Writers Project, part of the government-sponsored Works Progress Administration. The book is a compilation of black contributions from 1865 until 1940. It also listed the various exhibits on display at Chicago's 1940 Diamond Jubilee Exposition, which featured exhibits from every state, several Caribbean nations, and from Liberia.

Edited by Harlem Renaissance author Arna Bontemps and illustrated by Adrian Troy, an accomplished African American artist, *Calvalcade of the American Negro* is an important resource; it documents 75 years of black progress and is concrete evidence of the occurrence of an important black exposition in Illinois.

Today it is also a valued memorabilia item among collectors, as rare copies have begun to surface.

Cavalcade of the American Negro, 1940
Silkscreen poster by Cleo Sara
Prints and Photographs Division
LC-USZC2-1180

APRIL

1996: 43 African nations sign the African Nuclear Weapons Free Zone Treaty, pledging not to build, bury, stockpile, or test nuclear weapons.

monday
11

1966: Emmett Ashford becomes the first African American major league umpire.

1968: Black students occupy the administration building at Boston University and demand black history courses and admission of more black students.

tuesday
12

1907: Harlem Hospital opens in New York City.

wednesday
13

1775: The first US abolitionist society, the Pennsylvania Society for the Abolition of Slavery, is formed in Philadelphia by Quakers; Benjamin Franklin is its first president.

thursday
14

1889: Asa Philip Randolph, labor leader and civil rights advocate, is born in Crescent Way, FL.

1928: Norma Merrick (later Sklarek), first licensed African American female architect in the United States, is born in New York City.

friday
15

1864: Acclaimed singer Flora Batson is born in Washington, DC.

1973: Leila Smith Foley is elected mayor of Taft, OK, becoming the first black woman to serve as mayor of a US city. She will hold the position 13 years.

saturday
16

APRIL

s	m	t	w	t	f	s
					1	2
3	4	5	6	7	8	9
10	11	12	13	14	15	16
17	18	19	20	21	22	23
24	25	26	27	28	29	30

PALM SUNDAY

1758: Frances Williams, first African American to graduate from college in the Western Hemisphere, publishes a collection of Latin poems.

sunday
17

Harriet Tubman (American, c. 1822–1913)
Abolitionist, social reformer
Harriet Tubman, "the black Moses," was extremely committed—at great risk—to freeing slaves through the Underground Railroad. Fortunately, she had sufficient intuition, focus, and ingenuity to successfully execute her plans. It is estimated that Harriet Tubman delivered more than 300 slaves to freedom.

This brave revolutionary took many precautions to maintain the clandestine operation. She carried a firearm hidden under her skirt for use in rare cases when an escaped slave entertained thoughts about returning to the plantation.

This painting by Bernarda Bryson (Shahn) depicts another of Tubman's precautionary tactics—posing as a man while moving through society. Shahn was the artist wife of the famous American painter and photographer, Ben Shahn; in the mid-1930s they collaborated on the documentation of American rural life for the Resettlement Administration. A collection of images from that project was published in 1995 as *The Vanishing American Frontier: Bernarda Bryson Shahn and Her Historical Lithographs Created for the Resettlement Administration of FDR.*

Harriet Tubman escape, disguised as a man, 1934–1935
Ink and watercolor drawing by Bernarda Bryson (American, 1903–2004)
Prints and Photographs Division
LC-DIG-ppmsca-06782

April

PASSOVER (BEGINS AT SUNSET)
Independence Day (Zimbabwe)
1818: A regiment of Indians and blacks is defeated in the Battle of Suwanna, FL, ending the first Seminole War.

monday
18

Republic Day (Sierra Leone)
1938: Nana Annor Adjaye, Pan-Africanist, dies in West Nzima, Ghana.

tuesday
19

1926: Harriet Elizabeth Byrd is born in Cheyenne, WY. A teacher, in 1981 she becomes Wyoming's first black state legislator.
1984: Popular English vocalist Mabel Mercer dies in Pittsfield, MA.

wednesday
20

1966: PFC Milton Lee Olive is posthumously awarded the Medal of Honor for bravery during the Vietnam War.

thursday
21

GOOD FRIDAY
BANK HOLIDAY (CANADA, UK)
EARTH DAY
1526: The first recorded New World slave revolt occurs in what is now South Carolina.
1922: Bassist, composer, and bandleader Charles Mingus is born in Nogales, AZ.

friday
22

1856: Granville T. Woods, inventor of the steam boiler and automobile air brakes, is born.

saturday
23

APRIL

s	m	t	w	t	f	s
					1	2
3	4	5	6	7	8	9
10	11	12	13	14	15	16
17	18	19	20	21	22	23
24	25	26	27	28	29	30

EASTER
1993: Oliver Tambo, leader of the African National Congress, dies in Johannesburg.

sunday
24

Alexandre Dumas (French, 1802–1870)
Author
The literary genius Alexandre Dumas was a prolific novelist and playwright whose works were highly regarded in seventeenth-century French literature. Of his African ancestry, Dumas stated proudly, "When I discovered I was black I determined to so act that men should see beneath my skin." He strongly opposed slavery in America, writing to the Bishop of Autun, "There may even be relatives of mine who even now are forming part of the cargoes of slave vessels."

Fortunately, young Alexandre was inspired by his father and was blessed with a vivid imagination and an enviable memory. As a novelist, he excited readers with his intense portrayal of high drama, evident in his most popular fictional works, *The Three Musketeers, The Count of Monte Cristo,* and *The Man in the Iron Mask.*

Alexandre Dumas
Photographer: Goupil & Cie
Prints and Photographs Division
LC-USZ62-121730

APR • MAY

EASTER MONDAY (CANADA, UK EXCEPT SCOTLAND) *monday*
1918: Ella Fitzgerald, "First Lady of Song," is born in Newport News, VA.
1945: The United Nations is founded at a San Francisco meeting attended by W. E. B. Du Bois, Mary McLeod Bethune, Ralph J. Bunche, and Walter White.

25

1991: Maryann Bishop Coffey becomes the first female African American cochair of the National Conference of Christians and Jews. *tuesday*

26

1903: Maggie L. Walker becomes the first black woman to head a bank when she is named president of Richmond's St. Luke Penny Bank and Trust Company. *wednesday*
1994: South Africa's first all-races democratic elections are held.

27

1913: Political activist Margaret Just Butcher is born in Washington, DC. *thursday*
1957: Chicago lawyer W. Robert Ming is elected chairman of the American Veterans Committee, becoming the first black to head a major national veterans organization.

28

1854: Ashmun Institute (later Lincoln University), the world's first institution founded "to provide a higher education in the arts and sciences for youth of African descent," opens in Oxford, PA. *friday*
1992: Four Los Angeles police officers are acquitted of charges stemming from the beating of Rodney King; rioting ensues.

29

1951: Surgeons Rivers Frederick, Ulysses G. Dailey, and Nelson M. Russell are honored by the International College of Surgeons. *saturday*

30

MAY

s	m	t	w	t	f	s
	1	2	3	4	5	6	7
8	9	10	11	12	13	14
15	16	17	18	19	20	21
22	23	24	25	26	27	28
29	30	31				

1901: Poet, literary critic, and editor Sterling Brown is born in Washington, DC. *sunday*
1950: Gwendolyn Brooks becomes the first African American to win the Pulitzer Prize, for her book of poetry *Annie Allen*.

1

International Support for African Americans

In their struggle for equality, African Americans have received spirited support internationally. Many black activists became expatriates, changing their residences to Europe, Russia, Cuba, and many other parts of the world, reasoning that a different governmental system might be more equitable than what they saw as the capitalistic, unjust one that blacks were experiencing in America. The favorable treatment and respect they often received in their newly adopted countries confirmed their beliefs.

In the '60s, the writings of Mao Tse-tung, the Communist leader of the People's Republic of China, served as a revolutionary guide to alternative economic systems. While the Chinese were empathetic toward the struggles of African Americans, their support was also political one-upmanship, often practiced among rival superpowers.

Firmly Support American Blacks in Their Righteous Struggle!, 1963–1964
Poster by Yu-cheng Tsao
Prints and Photographs Division
yan 1a35986

MAY

BANK HOLIDAY (UK)

1969: Record-breaking cricket batsman Brian Lara is born in Santa Cruz, Trinidad.

monday

2

1855: Macon B. Allen becomes the first African American to be formally admitted to the bar in Massachusetts.

1902: Astride Alan-a-Dale, African American jockey Jimmy Winkfield wins his second Kentucky Derby in a row.

tuesday

● 3

1942: Songwriter Nickolas Ashford is born in Fairfield, SC. He and his wife, Valerie Simpson, will cowrite many pop hits.

1969: *No Place to Be Somebody* opens in New York. It will win the Pulitzer Prize the following year.

wednesday

4

CINCO DE MAYO

1905: Robert Sengstacke Abbott founds *The Chicago Defender*, calling it "the world's greatest weekly."

thursday

5

1995: Ron Kirk becomes the first black mayor of Dallas, with 62 percent of the vote.

friday

6

1941: Theodore Browne's play *Natural Man*, a production of the American Negro Theatre, premieres in New York City.

1946: William H. Hastie is inaugurated as the first black governor of the Virgin Islands.

saturday

7

MAY

s	m	t	w	t	f	s
1	2	3	4	5	6	7
8	9	10	11	12	13	14
15	16	17	18	19	20	21
22	23	24	25	26	27	28
29	30	31				

MOTHER'S DAY

1965: The Association for the Advancement of Creative Musicians is founded by Muhal Richard Abrams.

sunday

8

Captain Paul Cuffee (American, 1759–1817)
Atlantic trader, early African colonizationist
Paul Cuffee was born into a family with an entrepreneurial spirit and, from an early age, he was drawn to a career in business. His father was an ex-slave and a descendant of the great Ashanti Kingdom of seventeenth-century Ghana; his mother descended from the Wampanoag (People of the First Light), one of the original tribes to inhabit North America, predominantly in what is now the New England area.

Cuffee developed a strong interest in the maritime industry in his youth and learned all he could about ships, sailing, and navigation. At 16, he began to work on a whaling ship and then on cargo ships, eventually learning navigation and sailing techniques. With help from his brother David, Cuffee built his first three ships, began a cargo delivery business, and was on his way to becoming a wealthy man. The cargo business he began would amass a fleet of working ships, while consistently making huge profits for Cuffee.

Later Cuffee attempted to repatriate African Americans to Sierra Leone; though he invested much time and money, his attempts met with resistance and proved mostly unsuccessful.

Captain Paul Cuffee, 1812
Engraving by Mason & Maas
Prints and Photographs Division
LC-DIG-ppmsca-07615

MAY

1800: John Brown, abolitionist and martyr at Harpers Ferry, is born in Torrington, CT.

monday

9

1968: A public school in Brooklyn, NY, is named for noted scientist and inventor Lewis H. Latimer.

tuesday

◐ 10

1895: William Grant Still, dean of black classical composers, is born in Woodville, MS.

wednesday

11

1926: Mervyn Dymally, California's first African American lieutenant governor, is born in Cedros, Trinidad.

thursday

12

1914: Heavyweight boxer Joe Louis is born in Lexington, AL.

1990: George Stallings becomes the Black Catholic Church's first bishop. Stallings broke with the Roman Catholic Church in 1989, citing its failure to meet the needs of black Catholics.

friday

13

1913: Clara Stanton Jones, first black president of the American Library Association, is born in St. Louis, MO.

1969: John B. McLendon becomes the ABA's first black coach when he signs a two-year contract with the Denver Nuggets.

1999: Washington native Dolores Kendrick is appointed Poet Laureate of the District of Columbia.

saturday

14

MAY

s	m	t	w	t	f	s
1	2	3	4	5	6	7
8	9	10	11	12	13	14
15	16	17	18	19	20	21
22	23	24	25	26	27	28
29	30	31				

1918: PFCs Henry Johnson and Needham Roberts become the first Americans to win France's Croix de guerre.

1946: Camilla Williams appears in the title role of *Madama Butterfly* with the New York City Opera, becoming the first black female singer to sign with a major US opera company.

sunday

15

Ancient Egyptians and the Sphinx
The ancient Egyptians, with their highly developed society, colossal monuments to the pharaohs, burial practices, and other innovations, are considered one of the most advanced civilizations the world has ever known.

The sphinx pictured here may represent the Egyptian pharaoh Khufu (called Cheops by Western historians). He was the second king of Egypt under the 4th Dynasty, reigning approximately between 2590 and 2568 BC. The Great Pyramid and Sphinx of Giza, the most notable ancient monuments existing today, are truly "wonders of the world."

Upon seeing the sphinx, the French scholar Count Volney related, "There a people, now forgotten, discovered, while others were yet barbarians, the elements of the arts and sciences . . . now rejected from society for their sable skin and frizzled hair, founded on the study of the laws of nature, those civil and religious systems which still govern the universe."

Cairo. The Sphynx, between 1860 and 1890
Photographer unknown
Prints and Photographs Division
LC-USZ62-104866

MAY

1929: John Conyers Jr., founder of the Congressional Black Caucus, is born in Detroit.

monday

16

1954: The US Supreme Court declares school segregation unconstitutional in *Brown v. Board of Education*.

tuesday

○ 17

1946: New York Yankees baseball star Reggie Jackson is born in Wyncote, PA. He will set or tie seven World Series records.

1955: Mary McLeod Bethune, educator and founder of the National Council of Negro Women, dies in Daytona Beach, FL.

wednesday

18

1993: University of Virginia professor Rita Dove is appointed US poet laureate.

thursday

19

National Holiday (United Republic of Cameroon)

1868: P. B. S. Pinchback and James J. Harris are named the first African American delegates to the Republican National Convention.

friday

20

ARMED FORCES DAY

1833: African American students enroll in classes at the newly established Oberlin College in Oberlin, OH.

saturday

21

MAY

s	m	t	w	t	f	s
1	2	3	4	5	6	7
8	9	10	11	12	13	14
15	16	17	18	19	20	21
22	23	24	25	26	27	28
29	30	31				

1940: Bernard Shaw, journalist and principal Washington anchor for cable news network CNN, is born in Chicago.

1967: Noted poet Langston Hughes dies in New York City.

sunday

22

Dr. Kenneth B. Clark (American, 1914–2005)
Psychologist
Kenneth Clark grew up in Harlem, graduated from Howard University, and attended Columbia University, where he was the first African American to receive a doctorate in psychology.

In the 1950s Dr. Clark and his wife, Mamie, both psychologists, revealed the negative effects of school segregation on black children's self-esteem through their research. In his tests, Dr. Clark asked children, "Which doll is most like you?" while showing them black dolls and white dolls. Their responses overwhelmingly indicated a negative self-image.

The research carried out by the Clarks played a pivotal role in the Supreme Court ruling in *Brown v. Board of Education*. Kenneth Clark also contributed to Gunnar Myrdal's landmark book on racism, *An American Dilemma*, and he was the first African American to be elected president of the American Psychological Association.

Dr. Kenneth B. Clark conducting the "doll test"
Photographer: Gordon Parks
Prints and Photographs Division
LC-USZC4-4866

MAY

VICTORIA DAY (CANADA)

1832: Jamaican national figure Samuel Sharpe is hanged.

monday

23

1905: Distinguished educator Hilda Davis is born in Washington, DC.

1954: Peter Marshall Murray becomes president of the New York County Medical Society, the first African American physician to head an AMA affiliate.

tuesday

24

1963: African Liberation Day is declared at the conference of the Organization of African Unity in Addis Ababa, Ethiopia.

2009: Dr. Ivan Van Sertima, Guyana-born scholar, historian, and author of *They Came Before Columbus*, dies in Highland Park, NJ.

wednesday

25

1926: Renowned jazz trumpeter Miles Davis is born in Alton, IL.

thursday

26

1942: Dorie Miller, a messman, is awarded the Navy Cross for heroism at Pearl Harbor.

1958: Ernest Green becomes the first black to graduate from Central High School in Little Rock, AR.

friday

27

1981: Jazz pianist Mary Lou Williams dies in Durham, NC.

saturday

28

MAY

s	m	t	w	t	f	s
1	2	3	4	5	6	7
8	9	10	11	12	13	14
15	16	17	18	19	20	21
22	23	24	25	26	27	28
29	30	31				

1973: Tom Bradley becomes the first African American mayor of Los Angeles.

sunday

29

St. Martin de Porres (Peruvian, 1579–1639)
Friar

Martin de Porres was born out of wedlock in Lima, Peru. His father, Don Juan de Porres, was a Spanish nobleman and adventurer; his mother, Ana Velasquez, was a freed daughter of slaves from Panama. Don Juan abandoned his son and the mother of his child.

Martin's impoverished childhood left him with a special affinity for the poor in his community, and he was known to give to beggars what little he had.

As a Dominican friar, Martin devoted his life to serving God. He was known as the "flying brother," because he was often seen floating several feet above the floor of the chapel. Another of the miracles ascribed to him was bilocation: though he never left Lima, Peruvian merchants reported seeing him in places like Japan, Africa, and the Philippines. He was canonized by the Catholic church in 1962.

Design drawing for stained-glass window,
"Blessed Are the Merciful"
Designer: J. & R. Lamb Studios
Prints and Photographs Division
LAMB, no. 2069

MAY · JUN

MEMORIAL DAY
BANK HOLIDAY (UK)

1822: Denmark Vesey's conspiracy to free the slaves of Charleston, SC, is thwarted when Peter Prioleau betrays the plot to his master.

1965: Vivian Malone becomes the first black to graduate from the University of Alabama.

monday
30

1931: Mezzo-soprano Shirley Verrett is born in New Orleans. She will become world famous for her performance in *Carmen*.

1955: The US Supreme Court orders school integration "with all deliberate speed."

tuesday
31

National Day (Tunisia)

1919: Noted physician Caroline Virginia Still Wiley Anderson dies in Philadelphia.

wednesday
1

1948: Jamaican-born track star Herb McKenley sets a new world record for the 400-yard dash.

1999: Nelson Mandela's successor, Thabo Mbeki, is elected president of South Africa.

thursday
2

1904: Charles R. Drew, originator of blood plasma banks, is born in Washington, DC.

2009: Koko Taylor, "Queen of the Blues," dies in Chicago.

friday
3

1946: Legislation is enacted authorizing establishment of Mississippi Valley State University in Itta Bena.

1967: Bill Cosby receives an Emmy Award for his work in the television series *I Spy*.

saturday
4

JUNE

s	m	t	w	t	f	s
				1	2	3	4
5	6	7	8	9	10	11
12	13	14	15	16	17	18
19	20	21	22	23	24	25
26	27	28	29	30

Liberation Day (Seychelles)

1973: Doris A. Davis, mayor of Compton, CA, becomes the first African American woman to govern a city in a major metropolitan area.

sunday
5

Dorothy Maynor (American, 1910–1996)
Soprano, founder and director of the Harlem School of the Arts
With an angelic, dimpled face serenely carried on a petite frame, Dorothy Maynor thrilled audiences with her gifted voice—"a soaring, bell-like soprano capable of exquisite musical effects, supported by a sincere and ardent temperament," according to famed composer and conductor Nicolas Slonimsky.

Raised during a period of segregation, this Virginia native attended the Hampton Institute and sang in the choir. The school's choirmaster, R. Nathaniel Dett, noticed her vocal talent and encouraged her to become a soloist. She graduated in 1933 and then attended Westminster Choir College in Princeton, New Jersey. Afer her sensational New York debut in 1939, Maynor recorded her signature piece, "Depuis le jour" from Gustave Charpentier's *Louise,* in 1940.

In 1964 Maynor founded the Harlem School of the Arts in the basement of Saint James Presbyterian Church. From humble beginnings, the school became a powerhouse for talent; for example, Arthur Mitchell, one of the school's first ballet teachers, later cofounded the Dance Theatre of Harlem.

Dorothy Maynor
Photographer: Bernard Bruno
Prints and Photographs Division
LC-USZ62-102512

JUNE

1939: Marian Wright Edelman, the first female African American lawyer in Mississippi and founder of the Children's Defense Fund, is born in Bennettsville, SC.

monday

6

1917: Gwendolyn Brooks, US Poet Laureate and teacher, is born in Topeka, KS.

1994: The Organization of African Unity formally admits South Africa as its 53rd member.

tuesday

7

1939: Herb Adderley, Hall of Famer and defensive back for the Green Bay Packers, is born in Philadelphia.

1998: Nigerian military ruler Gen. Sani Abacha dies in the capital, Abuja.

wednesday

8

1877: Sculptor Meta Vaux Warrick is born in Philadelphia.

2000: World-renowned artist Jacob Lawrence dies from lung cancer in Seattle, WA.

thursday

9

1854: James Augustine Healy, first African American Catholic bishop, is ordained a priest in Notre Dame Cathedral.

1997: Geronimo Pratt, former Black Panther Party member, is released from jail after serving 27 years for a crime he did not commit.

friday

10

1964: Nelson Mandela is sentenced to life imprisonment by the South African government.

2000: Earl T. Shinhoster, prominent civil rights activist who led the NAACP through a difficult period, is killed in a car accident in Alabama.

saturday

11

JUNE

s	m	t	w	t	f	s
			1	2	3	4
5	6	7	8	9	10	11
12	13	14	15	16	17	18
19	20	21	22	23	24	25
26	27	28	29	30		

1963: Civil rights activist Medgar Evers is killed in Jackson, MS.

sunday

12

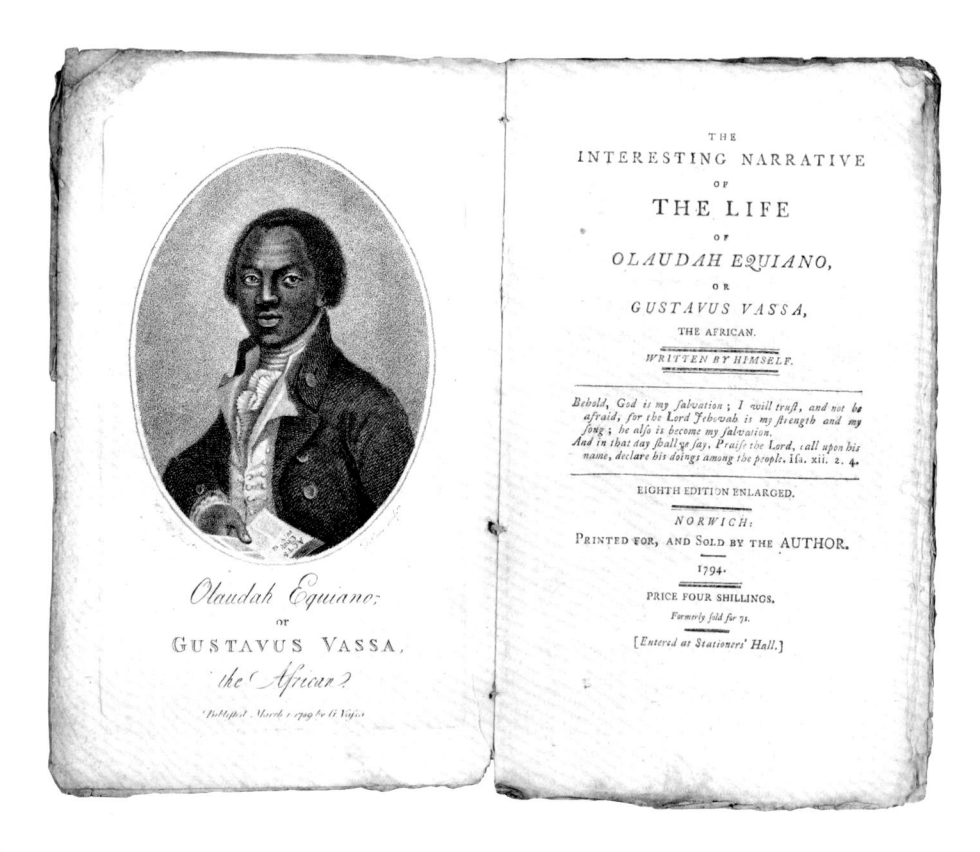

Olaudah Equiano (a.k.a. Gustavus Vassa) (African, 1745–1797)
Slave, author, abolitionist
When he was eleven years old, Olaudah Equiano was kidnapped from his home village in Africa and, after a period of servitude in a neighboring region, shipped to the West Indies. His first white owner was a Virginia planter; soon Equiano was bought by a British naval officer, Michael Pascal, who gave the young man to his cousins in London. The Guerin sisters insisted that the young man learn to read and write. By dint of scrupulous saving and canny investments over a decade, Equiano amassed enough capital to purchase his freedom.

In 1789 the 44-year-old Equiano wrote and published his autobiography, *The Interesting Narrative of the Life of Olaudah Equiano, or Gustavus Vassa, the African, Written by Himself*—a remarkable feat because the autobiography was not yet a well-developed genre. The former slave chronicled his life in vivid detail, from boyhood onward, and the result became a best seller in England and the United States. *The Interesting Narrative* is now recognized as the first book written in English by a former slave. A remarkable weapon in the fight to end slavery, the book also made its author a wealthy man.

Frontispiece and title page from *The Interesting Narrative of the Life of Olaudah Equiano*, 1794
Engraving by Daniel Orme, based on a painting by William Denton
Prints and Photographs Division
LC-USZ62-54026

JUNE

monday
1967: Thurgood Marshall is appointed to the US Supreme Court by President Lyndon B. Johnson.
1992: Dominique Dawes makes the US Olympic gymnastics team.

13

FLAG DAY

tuesday
1989: Congressman William Gray is elected Democratic whip of the House of Representatives, the highest leadership position in Congress held thus far by an African American.

14

wednesday
1927: Pianist and composer Natalie Hinderas is born in Oberlin, OH.

○ **15**

thursday
1976: Students riot in Soweto, South Africa.
1999: In Athens, Greece, Maurice Greene, US track and field athlete, breaks the 100-meter dash world record, running 9.79.

16

friday
1871: James Weldon Johnson, writer, poet, and first African American to be admitted to the Florida bar, is born in Jacksonville, FL.

17

saturday
1942: The US Navy commissions its first black officer, Harvard University medical student Bernard Whitfield Robinson.

18

FATHER'S DAY
JUNETEENTH

sunday
1865: News of the Emancipation Proclamation reaches the South and Texas through Gen. Gordon Granger.

19

Abram Petrovich Gannibal (Eritrean (?), 1696–1781)
Military engineer, civil servant
Abram Petrovich was an African prince who was brought to Russia and became a member of the court of Peter the Great. This cultural blend resulted in the many transliterations of his name: Gannibal, Hannibal, Abram, Ibrahim. Much that is known of his life appears in the book *Peter the Great's Negro,* written by his great-grandson, Alexander Pushkin.

Ibrahim, as he was known in Africa, was taken by Turkish slave traders and brought to Constantinople, then to Russia, where he made a great impression on Peter the Great, who informally adopted him. He received an excellent education and studied engineering and mathematics in France.

This education, and imperial favor, assured the young man a post in the Russian officer corps, where he rose to become the commander of Reval, a city in what is now Estonia. In 1762 he retired to his estate, where hundreds of serfs were in his thrall.

Abram Petrovich Gannibal
Artist: Boris Fedorovich Rybenhenkov
Prints and Photographs Division
LC-USZC4-14247

JUNE

National Holiday (Cameroon) — *monday*
1858: Charles Waddell Chesnutt, the first African American writer to win literary acclaim in the United States, is born in Cleveland.

20

SUMMER SOLSTICE 17:16 UTC — *tuesday*
1859: Renowned painter Henry Ossawa Tanner is born in Pittsburgh, PA.
1998: Marion Jones becomes the first athlete in 50 years to win the 100- and 200-meter events and long jump at the US Track and Field Championships in Indianapolis.

21

1972: National Black MBA Association is incorporated, with over 2,000 members.

wednesday

22

1899: Pvt. George Wanton is cited for bravery at Tayabacoa, Cuba, in the Spanish-American War.

thursday

23

1877: Bishop Josiah M. Kibira becomes the first black African leader of the Lutheran World Federation.

friday

24

National Day (Mozambique) — *saturday*
1792: Thomas Peters, an African American slave who led black emigrants from Nova Scotia to settle in Sierra Leone, dies in Freetown.
2009: Michael Jackson, "King of Pop," dies in Los Angeles.

25

JUNE

s	m	t	w	t	f	s
			1	2	3	4
5	6	7	8	9	10	11
12	13	14	15	16	17	18
19	20	21	22	23	24	25
26	27	28	29	30		

Independence Day (Madagascar and Somalia) — *sunday*
1993: Roy Campanella, legendary catcher for the Negro Leagues and the Los Angeles Dodgers, dies in Woodland Hills, CA.

26

Benin Bronzes

Benin sculpture has a rich historical tradition connected to the ancient high culture and advanced civilization known as Benin, which became Dahomey after French colonization in 1892. Upon gaining independence in 1975, the country was named the People's Republic of Benin; in 1990 the name changed to the Republic of Benin.

The early Benin civilization (which began around the early fourteenth century) was once a major trade and commerce center in West Africa. But after the arrival of French colonialists, Benin leaders capitalized on the Western demand for slave labor and were willing partners in the trade of fellow Africans until 1885.

The Benin bronze sculptures became famous and more valuable when their exquisite quality was realized. The widely used process of molding was known as "lost wax casting." Benin bronze pieces remain highly prized today.

The sculpture featured here depicts a king armed with a spear and sword, accompanied by two warrior bodyguards. Serving as an indication of the king's power, it was placed over the entrance to his residence.

Benin King and Two Attendants
Bronze relief
Photographer: John V. Twyman
Prints and Photographs Division
LC-USZC4-2141

JUN • JUL

National Day (Djibouti) — monday
1833: Prudence Crandall, a white woman, is arrested for teaching black girls at her academy in Canterbury, CT.
1872: Prominent poet and writer Paul Laurence Dunbar is born in Dayton, OH.

27

1911: Samuel J. Battle becomes the first African American policeman in New York City. — tuesday

28

Independence Day (Seychelles) — wednesday
1886: Photographer James VanDerZee is born in Lenox, MA.
1998: Atlanta Hawks head coach Lenny Wilkens becomes the second person to be elected to the NBA Hall of Fame twice, as a player and a coach.

29

Independence Day (Zaire) — thursday
1917: Actor, singer, and civil rights advocate Lena Horne is born in Brooklyn, NY.

30

CANADA DAY (CANADA) — friday
Independence Day (Burundi and Rwanda)
1899: Rev. Thomas Dorsey, father of gospel music, is born in Villa Rica, GA.
1975: Wallace D. Muhammad, head of the Nation of Islam, opens the group to members of all races.

● **1**

1908: Thurgood Marshall, first African American US Supreme Court justice, is born in Baltimore. — saturday
1999: Alexandra Stevenson, daughter of NBA star Julius Erving, is the first qualifier to advance to the semifinals of the Wimbledon tennis tournament in England.

2

JULY

s	m	t	w	t	f	s
					1	2
3	4	5	6	7	8	9
10	11	12	13	14	15	16
17	18	19	20	21	22	23
24	25	26	27	28	29	30
31						

1962: Jackie Robinson becomes the first African American to be inducted into the National Baseball Hall of Fame. — sunday

3

Kwame Nkrumah (Ghanaian, 1909–1972)
National leader
Kwame Nkrumah guided his country to independence from the United Kingdom (the two states are nearly identical in size) before becoming its first prime minister. Ghana is located on Africa's Gold Coast, the western region of the continent named by European colonizers for its abundant mineral resources and slaves.

Nkrumah's Western schooling (he attended elite schools in Ghana founded by Europeans, then attended college and graduate school in the United States and England) gave him a broad perspective on international politics, which became his passion. Fascinated by the struggles of African Americans for civil rights and of his fellow Africans for independence, he soon enrolled in the anticolonial enterprise.

In 1945 he worked with other activists to organize the Fifth Pan-African Congress, a powerful organization that permitted the people of the Gold Coast to challenge colonial referendums. In 1957, five years after he took charge of the government, Kwame Nkrumah led Ghana to independence from the United Kingdom.

First Inauguration in Ghana (Nkrumah Stands on Stool), 1960
Photographer: Associated Press
Prints and Photographs Division
LC-USZ62-112312

JULY

INDEPENDENCE DAY — *monday*
1881: Tuskegee Institute opens in Tuskegee, AL, with Booker T. Washington as its first president.

4

tuesday
1809: Eighteen blacks under the leadership of Reverend Thomas Paul establish the Abyssinian Baptist Church in New York City.
1892: Andrew Beard is issued a patent for the rotary engine.

5

Independence Day (Malawi) — *wednesday*
1993: Eleven lives are lost in an antigovernment riot in Lagos, Nigeria.

6

Saba Saba Day (Tanzania) — *thursday*
1993: Political violence in South Africa continues after the declaration of the nation's first all-races democratic election.

7

friday
1943: Women's rights advocate Faye Wattleton is born in St. Louis, MO.
2000: Venus Williams defeats Lindsay Davenport 6-3, 7-6, to win her first Wimbledon tennis championship.

8

saturday
1936: Poet and author June Jordan is born in Harlem, NY.

9

JULY

s	m	t	w	t	f	s
					1	2
3	4	5	6	7	8	9
10	11	12	13	14	15	16
17	18	19	20	21	22	23
24	25	26	27	28	29	30
31						

Independence Day (Bahamas) — *sunday*
1993: Kenyan runner Yobes Ondieki becomes the first man to run 10,000 meters in under 27 minutes.

10

The Black Panther Party

In the 1960s and 1970s the Black Panther Party took a stance against rampant police violence in the black community of Oakland, CA. Its activism was engendered to improve the lives of black people and the living conditions in black communities; the Panthers stressed education, economics, health, and self-sufficiency as well as self-defense against violent oppression, often perpetrated by the Oakland Police Department.

The Black Panther Party newspaper was the print medium that spread the word of the philosophy and events of the party. The most expressive and popular feature of the newspaper was the political art rendered by Emory Douglas (American, b. 1943), the paper's art director and the party's minister of culture.

Douglas's political vision, articulated through his art, is still remembered today. In addition to the 2007 book featuring a collection of his political cartoons, *Black Panther: The Revolutionary Art of Emory Douglas*, the artist has been honored through the mural *What We Want, What We Believe* at 122nd Street and Third Avenue in Harlem, New York.

Poster, 1970
By Emory Douglas
Prints and Photographs Division
LC-USZC4-10252

JULY

President's Day (Botswana)
1915: Mifflin Wistar Gibbs, first African American to be elected a municipal judge, dies in Little Rock, AR.

monday
11

BANK HOLIDAY (N. IRELAND)
1937: William Cosby, EdD, comedian, actor, educator, and humanitarian, is born in Philadelphia.

tuesday
12

1928: Robert N. C. Nix Jr., first African American chief justice of a state supreme court (Pennsylvania), is born in Philadelphia.

wednesday
13

1996: In Lapeenranta, Finland, Kenyan runner Daniel Komen shaves almost four seconds off the world mile record.

thursday
14

1929: Francis Bebey, guitarist and author, is born in Douala, Cameroon.

friday
○ 15

1882: Violette Anderson, first African American woman to practice before the US Supreme Court, is born in London.
1998: Dr. John Henrik Clarke, historian and scholar, dies in New York City.

saturday
16

JULY

s	m	t	w	t	f	s
					1	2
3	4	5	6	7	8	9
10	11	12	13	14	15	16
17	18	19	20	21	22	23
24	25	26	27	28	29	30
31

1911: Frank Snowden Jr., foremost scholar on blacks in antiquity, is born in York County, VA.

sunday
17

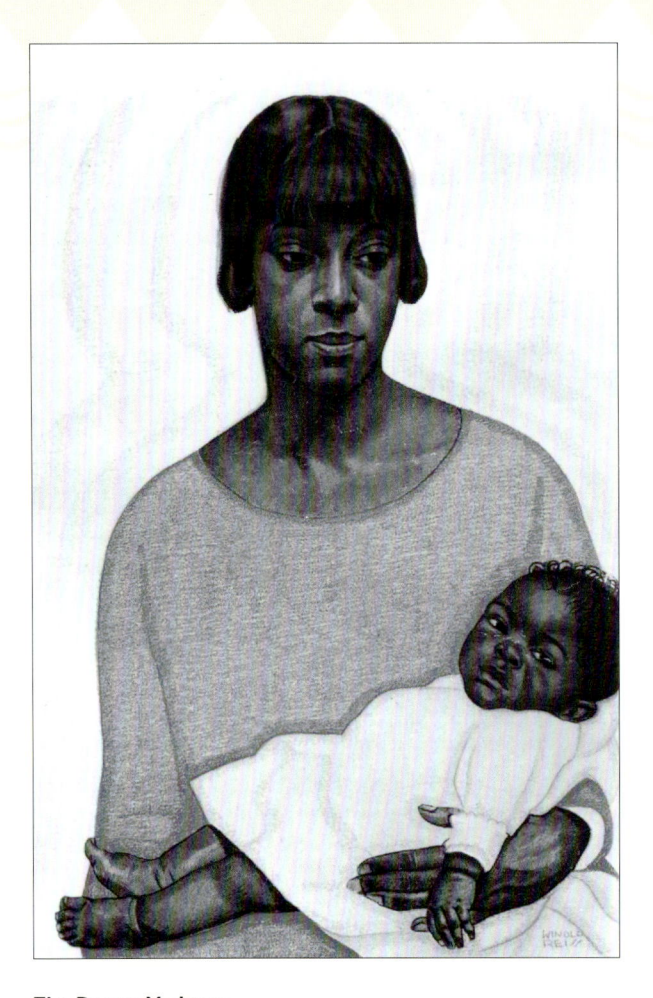

The Brown Madonna
The madonna and child, much like the Virgin Mary, is an important symbol of Christianity. In Europe there are numerous statues of the black madonna. This symbolism is also linked to the Egyptian goddess Isis, who is thought to be the origin of this concept.

Alain Locke (American, 1885–1954), a brilliant philosopher of the Harlem Renaissance period, attended Harvard University, and became the first African American to receive the prestigious Rhodes Scholarship to study in England at Oxford University. Locke employed Winold Reiss to illustrate his book, *The New Negro* (1925).

Born in Karlsruhe, Germany, Winold Reiss (1886–1953) traveled specifically to find the art subjects that interested him most. In America, Native American and African American cultures called to the artist, who relocated to the United States in 1913. His *The Brown Madonna* was included in Alain Locke's *The New Negro*.

The Brown Madonna, 1925
Halftone reproduction of painting by Winold Reiss
Prints and Photographs Division
LC-USZ62-52881

JULY

1896: First African American professional golfer, John Shippen, finishes fifth in the US Open.

1899: L. C. Bailey is issued a patent for the folding bed.

monday

18

1979: In her second Cabinet-level appointment, Patricia Roberts Harris is named secretary of health and human services.

tuesday

19

1967: The first National Conference of Black Power opens in Newark, NJ.

wednesday

20

1896: Mary Church Terrell founds the National Association of Colored Women in Washington, DC.

thursday

21

1939: Jane Bolin is appointed to New York City's Domestic Relations Court, becoming the first female African American judge.

friday

22

Anniversary of Revolution (Egypt)

1900: The first Pan-African Congress, organized by Henry Sylvester Williams, is held in London.

saturday

◐ 23

JULY

s	m	t	w	t	f	s
					1	2
3	4	5	6	7	8	9
10	11	12	13	14	15	16
17	18	19	20	21	22	23
24	25	26	27	28	29	30
31

1925: Operatic soprano Adele Addison is born in New York City.

sunday

24

Colonel Charles Young (American, 1864–1922)
Military leader, third African American to graduate from West Point
Born in Mays Lick, Kentucky, to former slaves, Charles Young entered the US Military Academy at West Point in 1884. Though ostracized and subjected to racial prejudice, he persevered and graduated in 1889. Young's military career began when blacks had only recently been allowed to serve and were still restricted to all-black regiments. During that period, the Tenth Cavalry and Twenty-fourth and Twenty-fifth Infantry divisions—regiments of the famed Buffalo Soldiers—earned respect when they rescued Theodore Roosevelt's Rough Riders at the battle of San Juan Hill. Young, in charge of a squadron of the Tenth Cavalry during the Spanish-American War, advanced to the rank of colonel in 1918, becoming the highest-ranking black in the US Army at the time.

In 1919 Young was appointed military attaché to the US embassy in Liberia, where he helped reorganize Liberian forces during that country's difficult adjustment to independence. He died while on a research expedition to Lagos, Nigeria, and was buried with military honors at Arlington National Cemetery. A 2003 biography by David Kilroy, *For Race and Country*, offers an in-depth review of Colonel Young's exemplary life and career.

Colonel Charles Young
Photographer unknown
Prints and Photographs Division
LC-USZ62-62353

JULY

1916: Wearing the protective mask he invented, Garrett Morgan enters a gas-filled tunnel with a rescue party after an underground explosion in Cleveland, OH; six lives are saved.

monday

25

Independence Day (Liberia)

1865: Catholic priest Patrick Francis Healy becomes the first African American to earn a PhD degree.

tuesday

26

1996: Donovan Bailey, a Jamaican running for Canada, becomes the "world's fastest human" in the Atlanta Olympics, setting a world record of 9.84 in the 100-meter dash.

wednesday

27

1868: The 14th Amendment is ratified, granting citizenship to African Americans.

1996: Ethiopian police officer Fatuma Roba becomes the first African woman to win a medal in an Olympic marathon.

thursday

28

1909: Crime novelist Chester Himes is born in Jefferson City, MO.

friday

29

1996: Three years after recovering from third-degree burns, Cuba's Ana Quirot wins a silver medal in the 800-meter run in the Atlanta Olympics.

saturday

● 30

JULY

s	m	t	w	t	f	s
					1	2
3	4	5	6	7	8	9
10	11	12	13	14	15	16
17	18	19	20	21	22	23
24	25	26	27	28	29	30
31						

RAMADAN (BEGINS AT SUNSET)

1921: Educator and civil rights activist Whitney Young Jr. is born in Lincoln Ridge, KY.

sunday

31

Bishop Desmond Tutu (South African, b. 1931)
Archbishop, activist
Desmond Mpilo Tutu was born in Klerksdorp, Transvaal, South Africa. The son of an educator, Tutu taught high school before he began his studies in theology. In 1975 he was the first black to be appointed dean of St. Mary's Cathedral in Johannesburg. He later served as bishop of Lesotho and was the first black general secretary of the South African Council of Churches.

Tutu's early activism centered on his nation's racist policies and the unjust imprisonment of Nelson Mandela; after apartheid was abolished, he served as chairman of South Africa's Truth and Reconciliation Commission. He has received numerous honors and awards, including several honorary doctorates, the Dalai Lama's Light of Truth Award, the Albert Schweitzer Prize for Humanitarianism, the Magubela Prize for Liberty, the Gandhi Peace Prize, and the Nobel Peace Prize.

Since his rise to prominence, Bishop Tutu has been a staunch supporter of justice for those less fortunate. He has championed the treatment and prevention of AIDS and support for survivors of natural disasters around the world; has spoken out against poverty, injustice, racism, sexism, and homophobia; and has consistently promoted peace among nations. Nelson Mandela, a friend of Tutu, said, "Sometimes strident, often tender, never afraid and seldom without humor, Desmond Tutu's voice will always be the voice of the voiceless."

Bishop Desmond Tutu
Photographer: Bernard Gotfryd
Prints and Photographs Division
LC-DIG-ppmsca-12455

AUGUST

CIVIC HOLIDAY (CANADA, MOST PROVINCES) — *monday*
BANK HOLIDAY (SCOTLAND)

Emancipation Day (Jamaica)

1996: At the Summer Olympics in Atlanta, Michael Johnson becomes the first man to win gold medals in both the 200- and 400-meter runs, breaking his own world record in the 200.

1

1847: William A. Leidesdorff launches the first steamboat in San Francisco Bay.

1997: Nigerian musician and political activist Fela Anikulapo-Kuti dies from AIDS in Lagos.

tuesday

2

Independence Day (Niger) — *wednesday*

1996: Josia Thugwane becomes the first black South African to win an Olympic gold medal, completing the marathon in 2 hours, 12 minutes, 36 seconds.

3

1961: Barack Obama, future president of the United States, is born in Honolulu.

1997: Australia's Cathy Freeman becomes the first aboriginal athlete to capture a world track title when she wins the 400-meter event in Greece.

thursday

4

1914: The first electric traffic lights (invented by Garrett Morgan) are installed in Cleveland.

friday

5

Independence Day (Jamaica) — *saturday*

1965: President Lyndon B. Johnson signs the Voting Rights Act, outlawing the literacy test for voting eligibility in the South.

◐ 6

AUGUST

s	m	t	w	t	f	s
	1	2	3	4	5	6
7	8	9	10	11	12	13
14	15	16	17	18	19	20
21	22	23	24	25	26	27
28	29	30	31			

1904: Ralph Bunche, first African American Nobel Prize winner, is born in Detroit.

sunday

7

Elisabeth Welch (American, 1904–2003)
Singer, actress
Elisabeth Welch was born in New York but made her name in London. Although she is relatively little known, this performer of the Harlem Renaissance period deserves equal status with such stars as Josephine Baker and Lena Horne.

Welch's Scottish-Irish mother encouraged her to sing, but her father, a devout man of African American and Native American heritage, vehemently opposed her vocation. She briefly pursued a career as a social worker but returned to singing.

Welch had a starring role in the black Broadway production *Runnin' Wild*, in which she popularized the Charleston, a dance that signified an era. Famous for her performance of "Stormy Weather," she appeared in numerous movies and theatrical productions in London and Paris and on Broadway.

After her retirement, Welch returned to the Broadway stage at the age of eighty-one, earning a Tony nomination for her performance in *Jerome Kern Goes to Hollywood;* in 1996 she sang "Stormy Weather" for a television documentary at the age of ninety-three. Her career is the subject of a 2005 biography by Stephen Bourne, *Elisabeth Welch: Soft Lights and Sweet Music.*

Elisabeth Welch
Photographer unknown
Prints and Photographs Division
LC-USZ62-138718

AUGUST

1865: Matthew A. Henson, first explorer to reach the North Pole, is born in Charles County, MD.

monday

8

1936: Jesse Owens wins four gold medals in track and field events at the Berlin Olympics.

2003: Gregory Hines, actor and dancer, dies from cancer in Los Angeles.

tuesday

9

1829: A race riot erupts in Cincinnati, prompting about 1,000 blacks to leave for Canada, Michigan, western Pennsylvania, and New York.

1989: Gen. Colin Powell is nominated as chairman of the Joint Chiefs of Staff.

2008: Isaac Hayes, singer, songwriter, and actor, dies in Memphis, TN.

wednesday

10

Independence Day (Chad)

1921: Alex Haley, author, is born in Ithaca, NY.

thursday

11

1890: Acclaimed soprano Lillian Evans Evanti, first African American to perform with an organized European opera company, is born in Washington, DC. In 1934 she gives a command performance for President Franklin Roosevelt at the White House.

friday

12

Independence Day (Central African Republic)

1989: The wreckage of the plane that carried US congressman Mickey Leland and others on a humanitarian mission is found on a mountainside in Ethiopia; there are no survivors.

2007: Educator and historian Asa Hilliard III dies in Cairo, Egypt.

saturday

○ 13

AUGUST

s	m	t	w	t	f	s
	1	2	3	4	5	6
7	8	9	10	11	12	13
14	15	16	17	18	19	20
21	22	23	24	25	26	27
28	29	30	31			

1990: Singer Curtis Mayfield is paralyzed in an accident at an outdoor concert in Brooklyn, NY.

sunday

14

Alessandro de' Medici (Italian, 1510–1537)
Duke of Florence
Many scholars believe that Alessandro de' Medici, the duke of Florence, was the first European ruler of African descent. His mother is thought to have been Simonetta da Collavechio, an African who served the prosperous and politically paramount Medici family as a domestic servant. His paternity is disputed: some opt for Clement VII (a Medici) and others for Lorenzo II de' Medici.

On January 5, 1537, Alessandro was murdered by a distant cousin named Lorenzino. The duke had reigned for five years, thanks to a scheme dreamt up by Pope Clement VII and Emperor Charles V. According to reports, Alessandro was lured into Lorenzino's house with the promise that awaiting him would be the beautiful Caterina, wife of Leonardo Ginori. While he waited, Alessandro fell asleep, and he awakened only as his assassins set on him with daggers.

A distant cousin, Cosimo I, avenged Alessandro's death by killing Lorenzino a year later, then assumed the throne.

Alessandro de' Medici
Portrait by Agnolo Bronzino
Prints and Photographs Division
LC-USZ62-35811

August

National Day (Republic of the Congo)

1938: Maxine Waters, second African American woman from California to be elected to Congress, is born in St. Louis, MO.

monday

15 227

Restoration Day (Dominican Republic)

1930: Innovative blues guitarist Robert Johnson dies in Greenwood, MS.

1998: Harlem Renaissance author Dorothy West dies in Boston.

tuesday

16 228

Independence Day (Gabon)

1993: Jackie Joyner-Kersee wins her 17th consecutive heptathlon at the World Track and Field Championships in Stuttgart, Germany.

wednesday

17 229

1963: James Meredith becomes the first African American to graduate from the University of Mississippi.

thursday

18 230

1989: Bishop Desmond Tutu defies apartheid laws by walking alone on a South African beach.

friday

19 231

1565: Black artisans and farmers aid the explorer Menendez in building St. Augustine, FL.

1619: The first group of 20 Africans is brought to Jamestown, VA.

saturday

20 232

AUGUST

s	m	t	w	t	f	s
	1	2	3	4	5	6
7	8	9	10	11	12	13
14	15	16	17	18	19	20
21	22	23	24	25	26	27
28	29	30	31			

1904: Bandleader and composer William "Count" Basie is born in Red Bank, NJ.

sunday

21 233

Fannie Lou Hamer (American, 1917–1977)
Civil rights activist
Seasoned by her early struggles—she was the youngest of twenty children and contracted polio in early childhood—and by years of sharecropping under the Mississippi sun, Fannie Lou Hamer (born Townsend) became a fearless stalwart of civil rights. She left school after the sixth grade to help her family in the cotton fields. In 1942 she married Perry "Pap" Hamer, also a sharecropper.

A mother of four, Hamer attended a meeting held by the Student Nonviolent Coordinating Committee (SNCC) in 1962. There she learned that African Americans could register to vote—and that injustices were being committed against them when they attempted to do so. After her own first attempt to register, Hamer was evicted from the plantation where she worked and lived. Attempts on her life followed, as did continuing death threats. She persevered, studying to pass the literacy test and paying the retroactive poll tax, and prevailed. However, she suffered immensely for her efforts, including being jailed and beaten so brutally that she incurred permanent vision and kidney damage. Undaunted, courageous, and outspoken, Hamer worked tirelessly with SNCC to educate and register black voters and went on to cofound the Mississippi Freedom Democratic Party and to organize food cooperatives and day care centers.

At the 1964 Democratic National Convention in Atlantic City, New Jersey, Hamer spoke powerfully of her personal journey. In fact, passage of the Voting Rights Act of 1965 by President Lyndon Johnson was influenced by the defiant words of Fannie Lou Hamer. Her most notable expression was "I'm sick and tired of being sick and tired."

Fannie Lou Hamer
Photographer: Warren K. Leffler
Prints and Photographs Division
LC-DIG-ppmsc-01267

AUGUST

1910: The famous Howard Theater in Washington, DC, opens for Broadway shows and musical entertainment.

1978: Kenyan president and revolutionary Jomo Kenyatta dies in Mombasa.

monday

22

1900: Booker T. Washington forms the National Negro Business League in Boston.

tuesday

23

National Flag Day (Liberia)

1903: Pianist and bandleader Claude Hopkins is born in Alexandria, VA

wednesday

24

1989: Huey P. Newton, cofounder of the Black Panther Party, dies in Oakland, CA.

thursday

25

1946: Composer, singer, and producer Valerie Simpson is born in the Bronx, NY.

friday

26

1937: Alice Coltrane, musician, is born in Detroit.

1963: W. E. B. Du Bois, scholar, civil rights activist, and founding father of the NAACP, dies in Accra, Ghana.

saturday

27

AUGUST

s	m	t	w	t	f	s
	1	2	3	4	5	6
7	8	9	10	11	12	13
14	15	16	17	18	19	20
21	22	23	24	25	26	27
28	29	30	31			

1963: A quarter million demonstrators take part in the March on Washington for Jobs and Freedom, the largest civil rights demonstration to date in US history.

sunday

28

Alexander Pushkin (Russian, 1799–1837)
Poet, author
Alexander Sergeyevich Pushkin, "the Father of Russian Literature," immortalized Russian folklore and profoundly influenced Russian culture and language. The scholar Henry Troyat remarked, "Other countries have . . . some one name that was the standard for a language and a people. In Russia it is Pushkin."

Pushkin's great-grandfather, Ibrahim Gannibal, was the son of an Ethiopian prince. At the age of eight, Gannibal was taken to Russia as a present for Peter the Great, who took an interest in the youngster and sent him to Paris to be educated. Gannibal eventually became a major general in the Russian army.

Born in Moscow, Pushkin spent much of his youth reading; by eleven he had read the French classics, and he published his first poem at fifteen. An independent thinker possessing a keen intellect, Pushkin repeatedly found himself in conflict with the government.

In Pushkin's day, the French language was preferred by Russian society; however, Pushkin boldly created his beautiful lines in Russian, using the language as nobody had done before. Among his most famous works are the narrative poem *The Bronze Horseman*, the dramas *The Stone Guest* and *Boris Godunov*, and a novel in verse form, *Eugene Onegin*. Today Pushkin is a symbol of pride in Russia and a revered figure in world literature.

Alexander Pushkin
Artist: Vasilli Andreevich Tropinin
Prints and Photographs Division
LC-USZC4-14396

AUG • SEP

BANK HOLIDAY (UK EXCEPT SCOTLAND) — *monday*
EID-AL-FITR (BEGINS AT SUNSET)
1920: Jazz saxophonist Charlie "Bird" Parker is born in Kansas City, KS.

29

Fête la rose (Feast of St. Rose of Lima), St. Lucia — *tuesday*
1983: Lt. Col. Guion S. Bluford Jr. becomes the first African American in space.

30

Independence Day (Trinidad and Tobago) — *wednesday*
1935: Baseball player and manager Frank Robinson is born in Beaufort, TX.

31

Heroes Day (Tanzania) — *thursday*
1993: Condoleezza Rice is named provost at Stanford University, becoming the youngest person and the first black to hold this position.

1

1833: Ohio's Oberlin College, first US college to routinely enroll black students, is founded. — *friday*
1975: Joseph W. Hatcher becomes Florida's first African American supreme court justice since Reconstruction.

2

1838: Frederick Douglass escapes from slavery, disguised as a sailor. — *saturday*

3

SEPTEMBER

s	m	t	w	t	f	s
				1	2	3
4	5	6	7	8	9	10
11	12	13	14	15	16	17
18	19	20	21	22	23	24
25	26	27	28	29	30	

1957: Arkansas governor Orval Faubus calls out the National Guard to bar African American students from entering a high school in Little Rock. — *sunday*

4

Heb. 13. 3.

PHŒBE.
Jamaica Royal Gazette, Oct. 7, 1826.
35—42   Spanish-Town Workhouse.
Notice is hereby given, that unless the undermentioned Slave is taken out of this Workhouse, prior to Monday the 30th day of October next, she will on that day, between the hours of 10 and 12 o'Clock in the forenoon, be put up to Public Sale, and sold to the highest and best bidder, at the Cross-Keys Tavern, in this Town, agreeably to the Workhouse Law now in force, for payment of her fees.

PHŒBE, a Creole, 5 feet 4½ inches, marked NELSON on breasts, and I O on right shoulder, first said to one Miss Roberts, a free Black, in Vere, secondly, to Thomas Oliver, Esq. St. John's, but it is very lately ascertained that her right name is Quasheba, and she belongs to Salisbury-Plain plantation, in St. Andrew's; Mr. John Smith is proprietor.   May 11

Ordered, that the above be published in the Newspapers appointed by Law, for Eight Weeks.
By order of the Commissioners,
T. RENNALLS, Sup.

" To admit *Slave-evidence* (of course cautiously and properly guarded) and to abolish the *whipping of women*, are two desirable points, and would destroy topics used with much effect against the Colonies."
Letter of J. R. Grosett, Esq. (a West India Proprietor,) to the Editor of the Jamaica Journal and Kingston Chronicle, August 1, 1826.

Phoebe—Slave Girl of Jamaica

It has been said that slaves in the Caribbean islands endured conditions less harsh than those in the southern United States. Slave owners were generally absent (most lived in England or France), and slaves in the islands outnumbered the hired hands: the picture offered is often of an idyll in paradise, days spent basking in sunshine as tropical fruits tumbled from the trees into delighted mouths.

This was not the case for Phoebe, a young slave in Jamaica, whose owners gave notice of her upcoming sale in the advertisement reproduced above. Those who drew up the ad had little regard for a slave's humanity. Phoebe is described as "Creole, 5 feet 4½ inches, marked 'Nelson' on breasts and 'I O' on right shoulder." Her first owner appears to have been "Roberts, a free black, in Vere." To us it might seem strange that blacks owned slaves, but in Africa the practice was ubiquitous.

Under British rule, slavery in Jamaica was abolished in 1834, close to 30 years before Abraham Lincoln's Emancipation Proclamation.

Phoebe
Print from *Jamaica Royal Gazette,* October 7, 1826
Prints and Photographs Division
LC-USZ62-65014

SEPTEMBER

LABOR DAY (US, CANADA) *monday*
1960: Leopold Sedar Senghor, poet and politician, is elected president of Senegal.

5 248

Independence Day (Swaziland) *tuesday*
1996: Eddie Murray joins Hank Aaron and Willie Mays as the only baseball players with at least 500 home runs and 3,000 hits.

6 249

Independence Day (Brazil) *wednesday*
1927: Dolores Kendrick, future Poet Laureate of the District of Columbia, is born in Washington, DC.

1954: Integration of public schools begins in Washington, DC, and Baltimore.

7 250

1766: Joseph Boulogne Saint-George participates in his first public fencing match in Paris. *thursday*

1981: Roy Wilkins, executive director of the NAACP, dies in New York City.

8 251

1915: Dr. Carter G. Woodson founds the Association for the Study of Negro Life and History. *friday*

1999: A Texas jury imposes the death sentence on Lawrence Russell Brewer, the second white supremacist convicted of killing James Byrd Jr.

9 252

National Day (Belize) *saturday*
1961: Jomo Kenyatta returns to Kenya from exile, during which he had been elected president of the Kenya National African Union.

10 253

SEPTEMBER

s	m	t	w	t	f	s
				1	2	3
4	5	6	7	8	9	10
11	12	13	14	15	16	17
18	19	20	21	22	23	24
25	26	27	28	29	30	

1974: Haile Selassie I is deposed from the Ethiopian throne. *sunday*

1999: 17-year-old Serena Williams defeats Martina Hingis to win her first major tennis championship, the US Open.

11 254

Pío Pico (Mexican, 1801–1894)
Last Mexican governor of California
Pío de Jesus Pico is well remembered throughout the Los Angeles metropolis. In addition to Pico Boulevard, Pío Pico State Historic Park, and the city of Pico Rivera, numerous city sites bear his name.

Pico was the fourth of ten children of mixed ancestry born to José María Pico and María Estaquia Lopez. In the 1790 census, his paternal grandmother, María Jacinta de la Bastida, was listed as "mulatto."

As a politician, businessman, and soldier, Pico was involved in the affairs of California and neighboring Mexico. He was uniquely situated in the region during the United States annexation, which he fought to prevent. Dejected, he was forced to flee to Mexico to avoid prosecution. Later he returned to California, gaining citizenship rights via the Treaty of Guadalupe Hidalgo. Upon his return, he built the first major hotel in Los Angeles, Casa del Pico, a three-story, thirty-three-room luxury facility.

Although the record is disputed, it is said that in 1845 Pico became the last Mexican governor of California after a "bloodless artillery duel" in an area near what is today Universal Studios.

Pío Pico
Photoprint by Schumacker, Los Angeles
Prints and Photographs Division
LC-USZ62-85205

September

Independence Day (Cape Verde)
1913: Track and field star Jesse Owens is born in Oakville, AL.
1977: Stephen Biko, leader of the black consciousness movement in South Africa, dies in police custody in Pretoria.

monday

○ 12

1913: Dancer, Tony Award winner, and famed Motown choreographer Cholly Atkins is born in Pratt City, AL.

tuesday

13

1980: Dorothy Boulding Ferebee, physician and second president of the National Council for Negro Women, dies in Washington, DC.

wednesday

14

1830: The first national convention for blacks is held at Bethel Church, Philadelphia.
1943: Paul Robeson performs in *Othello* for the 269th time.

thursday

15

Independence Day (Papua New Guinea)
1925: Blues great B. B. King is born in Indianola, MS.

friday

16

National Heroes Day (Angola)
1983: Vanessa Williams, Miss New York, becomes the first black Miss America.

saturday

17

SEPTEMBER

s	m	t	w	t	f	s
				1	2	3
4	5	6	7	8	9	10
11	12	13	14	15	16	17
18	19	20	21	22	23	24
25	26	27	28	29	30	

1980: Cosmonaut Arnoldo Tamayo, a Cuban, becomes the first black to travel in space.

sunday

18

Dr. Ralph Bunche (American, 1904–1971)
Diplomat, professor
We need a Ralph Bunche today, when peace is more important than ever to people around the world. Bunche was a visionary who worked his entire life for peace and goodwill among nations and individuals. His key role during the earliest years of the United Nations set the stage for implementing peaceful solutions to conflicts.

Born in Detroit, Bunche attended the University of California, Los Angeles, on an athletic scholarship, graduating with honors in 1927. He earned a master's degree in political science and a doctorate in government and international relations from Harvard University. During his training in social science, he traveled the world studying the institutions and customs of other countries.

Bunche played a major role in the formation of the United Nations. Dag Hammarskjöld, the second UN secretary-general, called Bunche the organization's "heart, brains, and right arm." As a key UN mediator in Palestine, Bunche negotiated an Arab-Israeli armistice—a nearly two-year process that won him the 1950 Nobel Peace Prize and world renown.

Dr. Ralph Bunche
Photographer: Sydney M. Schonbrunn
Prints and Photographs Division
LC-USZC2-2300

SEPTEMBER

1963: Iota Phi Theta fraternity is founded at Morgan State University, Baltimore.

1989: Gordon Parks's *Learning Tree* is among the first films listed on the National Film Registry of the Library of Congress.

monday

19

1664: Maryland takes the lead in passing laws against the marriage of English women to black men.

1830: The National Negro Convention convenes in Philadelphia with the purpose of abolishing slavery.

tuesday

20

INTERNATIONAL DAY OF PEACE

Independence Day (Belize)

1998: Florence "Flo-Jo" Griffith-Joyner, Olympic gold medalist in track, dies at 39 from an apparent heart seizure in Mission Viejo, CA.

2008: President Thabo Mbeki of South Africa resigns from office.

wednesday

21

Independence Day (Mali)

1828: Zulu leader Shaka the Great is assassinated.

1915: Xavier University, the first African American Catholic college, opens in New Orleans.

thursday

22

AUTUMNAL EQUINOX 09:04 UTC

1993: South Africa's parliament creates a multiracial body to oversee the end of exclusive white control of the nation.

friday

23

Republic Day (Trinidad)

1923: Nancy Green, the world's first living trademark (Aunt Jemima), is struck and killed by an automobile in Chicago.

saturday

24

SEPTEMBER

s	m	t	w	t	f	s
				1	2	3
4	5	6	7	8	9	10
11	12	13	14	15	16	17
18	19	20	21	22	23	24
25	26	27	28	29	30	

Referendum Day (Rwanda)

1911: Dr. Eric Williams, future prime minister of Trinidad and Tobago, is born in Port of Spain.

1974: Barbara W. Hancock becomes the first African American woman to be named a White House Fellow.

sunday

25

Miriam Zenzi Makeba (South African, 1932–2008)
Singer, civil rights activist
Ahmed Sékou Touré, former president of Guinea, called Miriam Makeba "the Empress of African Song." It is an apt title, for only an empress could have graced the stage for so many world leaders—including Jomo Kenyatta, Haile Selassie, Fidel Castro, François Mitterand, and John F. Kennedy—with such style, singing in many languages and dialects.

Makeba's reputation opened the doors of the international community. Her music was banned in her homeland, South Africa, from 1960 to 1990, but Makeba became a citizen of the world. In 1962 she addressed the United Nations Special Committee Against Apartheid. Makeba was awarded the Dag Hammarskjöld Peace Prize in 1986. In 1995 she performed for Pope John Paul II and toured Australia, Germany, Austria, and the United States.

Makeba was a social activist who literally performed until the end of her life. In 2008 she succumbed to a heart attack after singing her signature song, "Pata Pata," at a benefit concert in Italy.

Miriam Makeba is a registered trademark owned by the ZM Makeba Trust.
All rights reserved.
Photographer unknown
Prints and Photographs Division
LC-USZ62-138703

SEP • OCT

1937: Bessie Smith, "Empress of the Blues," dies in Clarksdale, MS. 1998: Betty Carter, jazz singer, dies from pancreatic cancer in New York City.	*monday* 26
1944: Stephanie Pogue, artist and professor, is born in Shelby, NC.	*tuesday* ● 27
ROSH HASHANAH (BEGINS AT SUNSET) 1829: David Walker, a freeborn black, publishes a provocative pamphlet calling for slaves worldwide to revolt against their white masters. 1912: W. C. Handy's "Memphis Blues" is published.	*wednesday* 28
1980: The Schomburg Center for Research in Black Culture opens a new $3.8 million building in New York City. 1997: Brazil mercifully agrees to accept thousands of African refugees fleeing war in Angola.	*thursday* 29
Independence Day (Botswana) 1935: Singer Johnny Mathis is born in Gilmer, TX.	*friday* 30
Independence Day (Nigeria) 1903: Virginia Proctor Powell, the first professionally trained female African American librarian, is born in Wilkinsburg, PA. 1996: Lt. Gen. Joe Ballard becomes the first African American to head the Army Corps of Engineers.	*saturday* 1

OCTOBER

s	m	t	w	t	f	s
						1
2	3	4	5	6	7	8
9	10	11	12	13	14	15
16	17	18	19	20	21	22
23	24	25	26	27	28	29
30	31					

1958: The Republic of Guinea, under Ahmed Sékou Touré, gains independence from France.

sunday
2

Isaac Murphy (American, 1861–1896)
Jockey
Called by racing experts the "greatest jockey in the history of the sport," Isaac Murphy dedicated his life to elevating the sport of horse racing to an art form.

Born January 1, 1861, in Kentucky, Murphy grew up in the saddle—grooming and working horses in the morning, training and exercising them in the afternoon, and accepting only nominal fees for his hard work and dedication.

Murphy won his first race on Glentina at the age of fifteen, and in 1884 he won his first Kentucky Derby on Buchanan, owned by William Bird, an African American. A second Derby victory on Riley in 1890 and a historic third win on Kingman in 1891 made Murphy the first jockey to ride winning mounts in the Derby three times and the first to win the prestigious race in two consecutive years. It is said that Murphy rode with his hands and his knees, raising the whip solely for the sake of the crowd.

Isaac Murphy
Photograph © Fenton
Prints and Photgraphs Division
LC-USZ62-50261

OCTOBER

1990: Rio de Janeiro's first black congresswoman, Benedita da Silva, sweeps the first round of the city's mayoral race.

monday

3

Independence Day (Lesotho)

1943: H. Rap Brown, chairman of the Student Nonviolent Coordinating Committee (SNCC), is born in Baton Rouge, LA.

tuesday

4

1878: George B. Vashon, first African American lawyer in the state of New York, dies in Rodney, MS.

wednesday

5

1917: Fannie Lou Hamer, founder of the Mississippi Freedom Democratic Party, is born in Montgomery County, MS.

thursday

6

YOM KIPPUR (BEGINS AT SUNSET)

1993: Author Toni Morrison becomes the first African American to win the Nobel Prize in literature.

friday

7

1820: Henri Christophe, leader of Haitian independence from France, dies in Cap-Haïtien.

1941: Rev. Jesse L. Jackson, political activist and civil rights leader, is born in Greenville, SC.

1980: Bob Marley collapses during a concert in Pittsburgh, PA; he will not perform again.

saturday

8

OCTOBER

s	m	t	w	t	f	s
						1
2	3	4	5	6	7	8
9	10	11	12	13	14	15
16	17	18	19	20	21	22
23	24	25	26	27	28	29
30	31					

Independence Day (Uganda)

1806: Mathematician and astronomer Benjamin Banneker dies in Ellicott City, MD.

sunday

9

Joseph Jenkins Roberts (Liberian, b. United States, 1809–1876)
President of Liberia
The state of Virginia, the birthplace of eight US presidents, is also the home of the first president of Liberia: Joseph Jenkins Roberts.

Roberts, the oldest of seven children, was born in Norfolk to Amelia and James Roberts, both free blacks who were among the most accomplished in Virginia. His mother was described as "a woman of intelligence, moral character, and industrious habits." His father established a boating business, transporting goods from Petersburg to Norfolk on the James River.

Roberts served six terms as president of Liberia, gaining worldwide respect and support for his country. In the capital city Monrovia, the citizens erected two monuments of Roberts to honor his achievements. The nation's main airport, Roberts International Airport (also called Robertsfield), and one of its most important coastal cities, Robertsport, are both named in his honor, as is Roberts Street in Monrovia.

Joseph Jenkins Roberts, c. 1851
Daguerreotype by Rufus Anson
Prints and Photographs Division
LC-USZC4-4609

OCTOBER

COLUMBUS DAY
THANKSGIVING DAY (CANADA)

1901: Frederick Douglass Patterson, founder of the United Negro College Fund, is born in Washington, DC.

1935: George Gershwin's *Porgy and Bess* premieres at Alvin Theater, New York City.

monday

10

1792: Antoine Blanc founds the first black Catholic order of nuns.

1919: Jazz drummer and band-leader Art Blakey is born in Pittsburgh, PA.

tuesday

11

1932: Comedian and civil rights activist Dick Gregory is born in St. Louis, MO.

wednesday

○ **12**

1902: Arna Bontemps, poet and librarian, is born in Alexandria, LA.

1925: Garland Anderson's *Appearances*, the first full-length Broadway play by an African American, opens at the Frolic Theater.

thursday

13

Young People's Day (Democratic Republic of the Congo)

1964: Dr. Martin Luther King Jr. is awarded the Nobel Peace Prize.

friday

14

1968: Wyomia Tyus becomes the first person to win the gold medal in the 100-meter race in two consecutive Olympic games.

saturday

15

OCTOBER

s	m	t	w	t	f	s
						1
2	3	4	5	6	7	8
9	10	11	12	13	14	15
16	17	18	19	20	21	22
23	24	25	26	27	28	29
30	31					

1995: The Million Man March, "A Day of Atonement," takes place in Washington, DC.

sunday

16

Wangari Maathai (Kenyan, b. 1940)
Environmentalist, human rights activist
Wangari Maathai was born in Nyeri, Kenya. She is a member of the Kikuyu tribe, Kenya's dominant ethnic group. Her education was spurred by prominent politician Tom Mboya's vision of providing Western education for Kenyans during the postcolonial period; an excellent student, Maathai was one of those chosen to study in the United States.

After earning a Master of Science degree from the University of Pittsburgh, she furthered her education in Germany. Back in Kenya, at the University of Nairobi, she earned a PhD degree in anatomy in 1971. This level of educational achievement was then unknown to the women of East Africa, distinguishing Maathai as a trailblazer.

Wangari Maathai has continued rising to new heights, and she has applied her success and political clout toward working for the benefit of humanity and the environment. Through implementation of her Green Belt Movement, she became an internationally recognized environmentalist. Also an outspoken human rights activist, Maathai was the first black woman to be awarded a Nobel Peace Prize (2004).

Wangari Maathai
Photograph courtesy Betty Press, Nairobi

October

Mother's Day (Malawi)
1806: Jean-Jacques Dessalines, revolutionist and emperor of Haiti, is assassinated in Port-au-Prince.

monday
17

1903: Félix Houphouët-Boigny, president of Ivory Coast, is born in Yamoussoukro.

1926: Rock 'n' roll legend Chuck Berry is born in St. Louis, MO.

tuesday
18

1878: Dr. Frederick Victor Nanka Bruce, the first physician on the Gold Coast, is born in Accra, Ghana.

1936: Dr. Johnnetta Cole, the first black female president of Spelman College in Atlanta, is born in Jacksonville, FL.

wednesday
19

1953: Jomo Kenyatta and five other Mau Mau leaders refuse to appeal their prison terms.

thursday
20

1872: John H. Conyers Sr. becomes the first African American admitted to the US Naval Academy.

friday
21

1936: Bobby Seale, cofounder of the Black Panther Party, is born in Dallas.

saturday
22

OCTOBER

s	m	t	w	t	f	s
						1
2	3	4	5	6	7	8
9	10	11	12	13	14	15
16	17	18	19	20	21	22
23	24	25	26	27	28	29
30	31					

1886: Wiley Jones opens the first streetcar line in Pine Bluff, AR.

sunday
23

Thomas-Alexandre Dumas (French, 1762–1806)

Thomas Dumas may have eclipsed the legacy of his famous literary son. In his five-volume *The Armies of the First French Republic,* historian Colonel W. R. Phipps stated that "even Alexandre Dumas the novelist could not do justice to the heroic exploits of his incredible father." And Thomas Dumas's exploits are found within the records of French military archives.

Thomas Dumas, a general in Napoleon's army, was noted for his sterling character and super-human strength. According to author Francis Henry Gribble, "He could grasp an overhead beam, while on horseback, and lift the horse off the ground by the grip of his riding muscles." Though Thomas was a skillful fighter who was fierce in battle, he loved people and detested unnecessary warfare.

When the army continued to terrorize the people of Egypt well after Egypt had succumbed, General Dumas protested. As punishment, Napoleon refused to retire General Dumas with full honors, cut his pension in half, and denied him pay uncollected while Dumas had been a prisoner of war.

Thomas-Alexandre Dumas
General Collections

OCTOBER

UNITED NATIONS DAY

1996: Robert M. Bell becomes the first African American to serve as chief judge of Maryland's court of appeals.

monday
24
297

Independence Day (Zambia)

1992: Vivian Dandridge, dancer and singer, dies in Seattle, WA.

tuesday
25
298

1899: Meta Vaux Warrick, African American sculptor, arrives in Paris to meet artist Henry Ossawa Tanner.

1962: Actor Louise Beavers dies in Los Angeles.

wednesday
26
299

1891: D. B. Downing, inventor, is awarded a patent for the street letter box.

1924: Actor Ruby Dee is born in Cleveland.

thursday
27
300

1981: Edward M. McIntyre is elected the first African American mayor of Augusta, GA.

friday
28
301

1949: Alonzo G. Moron of the Virgin Islands becomes the first African American president of Hampton Institute, VA.

saturday
29
302

OCTOBER

s	m	t	w	t	f	s
						1
2	3	4	5	6	7	8
9	10	11	12	13	14	15
16	17	18	19	20	21	22
23	24	25	26	27	28	29
30	31					

SUMMER TIME ENDS (UK)

1831: Slave rebellion leader Nat Turner is captured in Virginia.

1966: Huey Newton and Bobby Seale found the Black Panther Party for Self-Defense in Oakland, CA.

sunday
30
303

Richmond Barthé (American, 1901–1989)
Sculptor

Richmond Barthé, a largely self-taught and highly successful sculptor, was born in Bay St. Louis, Mississippi. His artistic talent became obvious at a young age. A Catholic priest, impressed with a painting Barthé had done for a church festival and disturbed because no local art school would accept black students, funded Barthé's education at the School of the Art Institute of Chicago. His first solo exhibition, at the Chicago Women's City Club in 1930, earned him a Julius Rosenwald Fellowship.

Among Barthé's commissioned works are *General Toussaint L'Ouverture,* a bust he created for the Lake County Children's Home at Gary, Indiana; a memorial for James Weldon Johnson; and *Mother and Son*, which he produced for the New York World's Fair. Barthé is best known for his portrait busts of stage celebrities and important historical figures. His work has been exhibited widely in major art museums in the United States and abroad.

African American man beating a small drum, between 1930 and 1950
Sculpture by Richmond Barthé
Photographer: A. B. Bogart
Prints and Photographs Division
LC-USZ62-36617

Oct • Nov

HALLOWEEN
1900: Actor and singer Ethel Waters is born in Chester, PA.

monday
31

National Day (Antigua)
1945: John H. Johnson publishes the first issue of *Ebony*.
1999: Chicago Bears Hall of Fame running back Walter "Sweetness" Payton succumbs to liver disease in South Barrington, IL.

tuesday
1

1983: President Ronald Reagan signs a law designating the third Monday in January as Martin Luther King Jr. Day.
1996: Toni Stone, the first woman to play baseball in the Negro Leagues, dies in Alameda, CA.

wednesday
2

National Day (Dominica)
Independence Day (Panama)
1983: Jesse Jackson announces his candidacy for the office of president of the United States.

thursday
3

1992: Carol Moseley Braun becomes the first African American woman to be elected to the US Senate.
2008: Barack Obama becomes the first African American elected president of the United States.

friday
4

EID-AL-ADHA (BEGINS AT SUNSET)
1862: Frazier A. Boutelle is commissioned as a second lieutenant in the 5th New York Cavalry.

saturday
5

NOVEMBER

s	m	t	w	t	f	s
		1	2	3	4	5
6	7	8	9	10	11	12
13	14	15	16	17	18	19
20	21	22	23	24	25	26
27	28	29	30			

DAYLIGHT SAVING TIME ENDS
Green March Day (Morocco)
1983: Sgt. Farley Simon, a native of Grenada, becomes the first marine to win the Marine Corps Marathon.
1989: Renowned attorney Sadie Tanner Mossell Alexander dies in Philadelphia.

sunday
6

Queen Charlotte Sophia (British, 1744–1818)
Queen consort of King George III

Finding a true likeness of Queen Charlotte Sophia among her numerous portraits is a challenge. As much as her British subjects desired her appearance to be completely in the tradition of preceding queens, she was different. Consequently, most of the painters she sat for tended to "Europeanize" her image, painting her to fit the European conception of beauty. Only Allan Ramsay, the son of an abolitionist, and a staunch anti-slavery activist himself, painted the queen in her true likeness, disregarding the British tradition.

Historian and author, Mario de Valdes y Cocom, suggested that Ramsay intentionally emphasized the features of the queen that reflected her African ancestry. Valdes states, "Queen Charlotte descended from Margarita de Castro y Sousa, a black member of the Portuguese Royal House. The queen's personal physician, Baron Stockmar, describes her as 'having a true mulatto face'" in a biography of the queen.

Queen Charlotte of England
Portrait by Allan Ramsay (Scottish, 1713–1784)
General Collections

November

1989: Douglas Wilder of Virginia becomes the nation's first black governor since Reconstruction.

monday

7

1938: Crystal Bird Fauset of Pennsylvania becomes the first African American woman to be elected to a state legislature.

tuesday

8

1731: Benjamin Banneker, scientist and inventor, is born in Ellicott City, MD.

1997: The NBA announces it has hired Dee Kantner and Violet Palmer, the first women to officiate in an all-male major sports league.

wednesday

9

1917: Musician and writer Nora Holt joins *The Chicago Defender* as the writer of the feature article "Cultivating Symphony Concerts."

1995: Nigerian author and poet Ken Saro-Wiwa is executed in Port Harcourt.

2008: Miriam Makeba, "Empress of African Song," dies in southern Italy.

thursday

○ 10

VETERANS DAY
REMEMBRANCE DAY (CANADA)
Independence Day (Angola)
1989: The Civil Rights Memorial in Montgomery, AL, is dedicated.

friday

11

1922: Sigma Gamma Rho sorority is organized by Mary Lou Allison and six other teachers at Butler University.

1941: Madame Lillian Evanti and Mary Cardwell Dawson establish the National Negro Opera Company.

saturday

12

NOVEMBER

s	m	t	w	t	f	s
		1	2	3	4	5
6	7	8	9	10	11	12
13	14	15	16	17	18	19
20	21	22	23	24	25	26
27	28	29	30			

1940: In *Hansberry v. Lee* the Supreme Court rules that African Americans cannot be barred from white neighborhoods.

1998: Kenny Kirkland, jazz pianist with the Branford Marsalis band, dies at home in Queens, NY.

sunday

13

Lucy Parsons (American, c. 1853–1942)
Labor activist, writer

Lucy Parsons was a lifelong advocate for the labor rights, socialist, and anarchist movements fomenting in Chicago during the late nineteenth and early twentieth centuries. She was the first black woman to become strongly committed to leftist activities and she spoke out on behalf of poor and homeless people of color in the United States.

Born in Waco, Texas, she later learned to disguise her racial identity by modifying her surname to names that suggested Native American or Mexican ancestry. She married a white ex-Confederate army scout, Albert Parsons; the couple soon left Texas and moved to Chicago, where they immersed themselves into the revolutionary movements and supported labor protests in the Haymarket affair. For his participation in the latter, Albert Parsons was—some say unjustly—executed with other activists. This event marked the beginning of May Day rallies around the world.

Lucy Parsons: American Revolutionary, 1976
Poster
Prints and Photographs Division
LC-USZ62-107189

November

monday
14

Children's Day (India)
1954: Dr. James Joshua Thomas is installed as minister of the Mott Haven Reformed Church in the Bronx, NY.

tuesday
15

218 BC: Hannibal crosses the Alps with 37 elephants and 26,000 men to defeat Roman armies at the Ticino and Trebbia rivers.

1998: Kwame Ture (Stokely Carmichael) succumbs to prostate cancer in Conakry, Guinea.

wednesday
16

1873: W. C. Handy, father of the blues, is born in Florence, AL.

thursday
17

1911: Omega Psi Phi fraternity is founded at Howard University.

1980: WHMM-TV in Washington, DC, becomes the first African American public-broadcasting television station.

friday
18

Independence Day (Morocco)
1900: Dr. Howard Thurman, theologian, educator, and civil rights leader, is born in Daytona Beach, FL.

saturday
19

Discovery Day (Puerto Rico)
1797: Abolitionist and women's rights advocate Sojourner Truth is born in Ulster County, NY.

1997: Drs. Paula Mahone and Karen Drake head a team of forty specialists in the first successful delivery of septuplets, born in Carlisle, IA.

NOVEMBER

s	m	t	w	t	f	s
		1	2	3	4	5
6	7	8	9	10	11	12
13	14	15	16	17	18	19
20	21	22	23	24	25	26
27	28	29	30			

sunday
20

1695: Zumbi dos Palmares, Brazilian leader of a 100-year-old rebel slave group, is killed in an ambush.

Joseph Boulogne (Chevalier de Saint-George) (French, b. Guadeloupe, 1739–1799)
Composer, violinist

France was the model for European culture during the eighteenth century. Even with revolution on the horizon, the French were masters of the fine arts of music, painting, dance, literature, and drama.

One notable Frenchman from this period was Joseph Boulogne Saint-George, born on the Caribbean island of Guadeloupe to an African slave mother and a French father. At thirteen, then living in France, Saint-George began studying fencing under the "master of arms," La Boessiere. Focusing primarily on physical training and academic studies in his early school years, Saint-George later became proficient with the violin and music composition.

A prolific composer, Saint-George created eleven symphonies, several operas, twelve string quartets, ten violin concertos, and other instrumental and vocal works. He was also an expert swordsman, swimmer, boxer, and the colonel of an all-black regiment during the revolution.

Monsieur de St. George
Engraving by Mather Brown
Photo courtesy IOKTS Archive

November

monday 21
1866: Duse Mohammed Effendi, Egyptian Pan-Africanist, is born.
1893: Granville T. Woods, inventor, patents the electric railway conduit.

tuesday 22
1994: Jazz musicians Herbie Hancock, Clark Terry, and Joshua Redman perform in a concert beamed by satellite to 60 schools nationwide.

wednesday 23
1941: Musician and actor Henrietta Vinton Davis dies in Washington, DC.

thursday 24
THANKSGIVING
National Holiday (Democratic Republic of the Congo)
Independence Day (Zambia)
1868: Scott Joplin, composer of ragtime music, is born in Texarkana, TX.

friday 25
MUHARRAM (BEGINS AT SUNSET)
Independence Day (Suriname)
1955: The Interstate Commerce Commission bans segregation in interstate travel.

saturday 26
1878: Marshall Walter "Major" Taylor, world's fastest bicycle racer for 12 years, is born in Indianapolis.
1927: Marcus Garvey, Pan-Africanist, is released from Tombs Atlanta Penitentiary.

sunday 27
1942: Rock musician Jimi Hendrix is born in Seattle, WA.

NOVEMBER

s	m	t	w	t	f	s
		1	2	3	4	5
6	7	8	9	10	11	12
13	14	15	16	17	18	19
20	21	22	23	24	25	26
27	28	29	30			

Empress Zauditu (Ethiopian, 1876–1930)
Empress of Ethiopia, 1916–1930
Empress Zauditu was the eldest daughter of Menelik II, who proclaimed himself a direct descendant of the royal union between Queen Sheba and King Solomon. In 1896, Menelik II led Ethiopia to a stunning victory over Italy, retaining Ethiopian independence.

Zauditu was the first woman to become head of state in modern Ethiopia, but she shared power with the renowned Ethiopian emperor, Haile Selassie, who was also appointed regent and heir apparent to the throne. Empress Zauditu became known for her strict religious convictions. Haile Selassie is most noted for leading Ethiopia into the modern world.

In 1924, Marcus Garvey, founder and leader of the Universal Negro Improvement Association, spoke of the Empress Zauditu in his convention speech, saying, "We hope for you and your country a reign of progress and happiness. Our desire is to help you maintain the glory of Ethiopia."

H. I. M. Empress Zauditu
Photographer unknown
Prints and Photographs Division
LC-USZ62-60869

Nov · Dec

monday
28

Independence Day (Mauritania)
1961: Ernie Davis becomes the first African American to win the Heisman Trophy.

---

tuesday
29

1908: Adam Clayton Powell Jr., politician and civil rights activist, is born in New Haven, CT.

---

wednesday
30

ST. ANDREW'S DAY (SCOTLAND)

Independence Day (Benin)
1912: Gordon Parks, filmmaker and photographer, is born in Fort Scott, KS.

---

thursday
1

1955: Rosa Parks defies the segregated transportation ordinance in Montgomery, AL, igniting a 382-day bus boycott and launching the civil rights movement in America.

---

friday
2

1968: Dial Press publishes Frank Yerby's *Judas My Brother*.
2008: Odetta Holmes, folk singer and civil rights activist, dies in New York City.

---

saturday
3

1911: Distinguished educator and historian Helen Gray Edmonds is born in Lawrenceville, VA.

---

sunday
4

1906: Alpha Phi Alpha fraternity, the first Greek organization for African Americans, is founded at Cornell University.

DECEMBER

s	m	t	w	t	f	s
				1	2	3
4	5	6	7	8	9	10
11	12	13	14	15	16	17
18	19	20	21	22	23	24
25	26	27	28	29	30	31

E. R. Braithwaite (Guyanese, b. 1920)
Writer, teacher, diplomat

Edward Ricardo Braithwaite was born in Georgetown, Guyana, and grew up in a privileged family. Since his mother and father graduated from the prestigious Oxford University in London, education was understood to be important for success in life.

Braithwaite's formal education was completed at City College of New York and Cambridge University, where he earned a doctorate in physics. But Braithwaite was unable to find employment in his field due to discrimination, so he settled for a teaching job in London. This experience led to him to write *To Sir, with Love*, a novel that became a movie classic as well as a Billboard No. 1 single of the same name (performed by the London artist Lulu). The lead role in the film was played by a young Sidney Poitier. In the film, black and white racial relations are exposed; despite initial conflicts, the end result is overwhelmingly positive.

In the late 1960s Braithwaite served as the Guyanese ambassador to Venezuela and as a representative to the United Nations.

E. R. Braithwaite
Photographer: Carl Van Vechten
Prints and Photographs Division
LC-USZ62-117467

December

1870: Alexandre Dumas (père), French novelist and dramatist, dies in Puys, France.

monday

5 ₃₃₉

1960: Some 500 store owners in Tucson, AZ, sign pledges vowing not to discriminate on the basis of race, color, or religion.

1997: Lee Brown defeats Rob Mosbacher to become Houston's first black mayor.

tuesday

6 ₃₄₀

Independence Day (Ivory Coast)

1941: Dorie Miller, a messman, downs three Japanese planes in the attack on Pearl Harbor.

1942: Reginald F. Lewis, owner of the first privately held African American Fortune 500 company, is born in Baltimore, MD.

wednesday

7 ₃₄₁

1850: Lucy Ann Stanton of Cleveland graduates from Oberlin College with a BA in literature.

1987: Kurt Schmoke becomes the first African American mayor of Baltimore.

thursday

8 ₃₄₂

Independence Day (Tanzania)

1919: Roy DeCarava, the first African American photographer to be awarded a Guggenheim Fellowship, is born in New York City.

friday

9 ₃₄₃

Human Rights Day (Guinea)

Independence Day (Panama)

1950: Dr. Ralph J. Bunche becomes the first African American to win the Nobel Peace Prize.

saturday

○ 10 ₃₄₄

DECEMBER

s	m	t	w	t	f	s
				1	2	3
4	5	6	7	8	9	10
11	12	13	14	15	16	17
18	19	20	21	22	23	24
25	26	27	28	29	30	31

Republic Day (Burkina Faso)

1926: Blues singer Willie Mae "Big Mama" Thornton is born in Montgomery, AL.

sunday

11 ₃₄₅

The Olmec

The Olmec, who beginning around 1200 BC populated coastal regions on the gulf side of what is now southern Mexico and Guatemala, produced several colossal (up to nine feet tall) stone heads with carved faces that provide clues about them. Pioneer anthropologist and linguist Dr. Ivan Van Sertima spent his lifetime studying this civilization. His findings revealed an African influence reflected in their writings, social practices, Christopher Columbus's diary, and their art, particularly the colossal heads. Van Sertima wrote in his compelling book, *They Came Before Columbus* (1976): "Some historians and archaeologists believe that a major cultural influence originating in Africa made its way across the Atlantic and created this cultural impetus."

The head featured here is from Tres Zapotes, Mexico, and dated around 800 BC. Van Sertima states, "This colossal stone head of Tres Zapotes is most convincing of the presence of Africans in the New World." In addition to the African features of this head, the back shows seven braids dangling over the headdress, a common hairstyle among people of African descent.

Predating both the Aztec and Maya, the Olmec represent the first Mesoamerican culture; they vanished around 300 BC.

Olmec Head, Tres Zapotes, Mexico
Photographer unknown
Courtesy Dr. Ivan Van Sertima

December

Independence Day (Kenya)

1995: Willie Brown defeats incumbent Frank Jordan to become the first African American mayor of San Francisco.

monday
12 346

1957: Daniel A. Chapman becomes Ghana's first ambassador to the United States.

1998: Former light-heavyweight boxing champion Archie Moore dies in San Diego, CA.

tuesday
13 347

1963: Dinah Washington, "Queen of the Blues," dies in Detroit.

wednesday
14 348

1883: William A. Hinton, developer of the Hinton test for diagnosing syphilis, is born in Chicago.

thursday
15 349

1976: President Jimmy Carter appoints Andrew Young ambassador to the United Nations.

friday
16 350

1760: Deborah Sampson Gannett, who will disguise herself as a man in order to fight in the Revolutionary War, is born in Plymouth, VA.

saturday
17 351

DECEMBER

s	m	t	w	t	f	s
				1	2	3
4	5	6	7	8	9	10
11	12	13	14	15	16	17
18	19	20	21	22	23	24
25	26	27	28	29	30	31

Republic Day (Niger)

1912: Gen. Benjamin O. Davis Jr. is born in Washington, DC.

sunday
18 352

Adah Isaacs Menken (American, 1835–1868)
Actress, painter, poet
Born of mixed parentage in New Orleans, Adah Bertha Theodore was considered a Creole, meaning "of mixed race" (usually black and white). This descriptor was commonly applied to the offspring of interracial marriages in Louisiana, particularly in New Orleans. In 1856 she married Alexander Isaacs Menken, whose name she retained after their divorce.

As a performer, Menken achieved fame primarily in San Francisco, where she preceded the reign of the great operatic diva Luisa Tetrazzini (1871–1941). Although Menken may have been deceptive regarding her heritage, it has been confirmed that she possessed an exceptional intellect, was a talented dancer, was fluent in Spanish and French, wrote brilliant poetry, and was an accomplished painter. She was courted by Alexandre Dumas père, among many others, and counted Charles Dickens among her friends. Her most famous role was in *Mazeppa*, an opera based on a poem by Alexander Pushkin.

Highly regarded in France, Adah Isaacs Menken was buried in the Montparnasse Cemetery, the final resting place of France's elite artists and authors.

Adah Isaacs Menken
Photographer unknown
Prints and Photographs Division
LC-USZ62-52371

December

monday
1933: Acclaimed actor Cicely Tyson is born in New York City.
19 353

tuesday
HANUKKAH (BEGINS AT SUNSET)
1988: Max Robinson, first African American news anchor for a major television network, dies in Washington, DC.
20 354

wednesday
1911: Josh Gibson, Negro Leagues home run king, is born in Buena Vista, GA.
21 355

thursday
WINTER SOLSTICE 05:30 UTC
1883: Arthur Wergs Mitchell, first African American elected to Congress, is born in Lafayette, AL.
1898: Chancellor Williams, historian and author of *The Destruction of Black Civilization*, is born in Bennettsville, SC.
22 356

friday
1867: Madam C. J. Walker, first female African American millionaire, is born in Delta, LA.
23 357

saturday
1853: Author and teacher Octavia Victoria Rogers Albert is born in Oglethorpe, GA.
● **24** 358

DECEMBER

s	m	t	w	t	f	s
				1	2	3
4	5	6	7	8	9	10
11	12	13	14	15	16	17
18	19	20	21	22	23	24
25	26	27	28	29	30	31

sunday
CHRISTMAS
1907: Cab Calloway, bandleader and first jazz singer to sell a million records, is born in Rochester, NY.
25 359

Ira Aldridge (American, 1807–1867)
Shakespearean actor

Ira Aldridge was born in New York City and attended the African Free School. Shortly thereafter, he joined an African theater company, honing his abilities on the stage until the troupe disbanded. Aldridge then emigrated to England, where his stage persona was established. He first appeared in *The Revolt of Surinam*, playing a slave, but his following performances as Othello brought him phenomenal fame and recognition. Though Othello was his signature role, Aldridge also gave tremendous performances as Hamlet, Macbeth, and King Lear.

In addition to Shakespearean roles, Aldridge staged an educational one-man program that he called "Grant Classic and Dramatic Entertainment," in which he performed excerpts from plays and presented lectures on drama.

Aldridge, the "African Roscius," toured Europe and Russia and was honored by several governments there, as well as by the government of Haiti. The main performance space for the Howard University Departmnent of Theatre Arts is the Ira Aldridge Theatre.

Ira Aldridge
Engraving by the London Printing and Publishing Company
Prints and Photographs Division
LC-USZ62-39869

Dec • Jan

CHRISTMAS HOLIDAY
BOXING DAY (CANADA, UK)

Kwanzaa begins: Umoja (Unity). *To strive for a principled and harmonious togetherness in the family, community, nation, and world African community.*

2009: Percy Sutton, attorney and politician, dies in New York.

monday
26

BANK HOLIDAY (UK)

Kujichagulia (Self-Determination). *To define ourselves, name ourselves, create for ourselves, and speak for ourselves.*

tuesday
27

Ujima (Collective Work and Responsibility). *To build and maintain our community together; to make our sisters' and brothers' problems our problems and to solve them together.*

wednesday
28

Ujamaa (Cooperative Economics). *To build our own businesses, control the economics of our own communities, and share in all our communities' work and wealth.*

thursday
29

Nia (Purpose). *To make our collective vocation the building and development of our community; to restore our people to their traditional greatness.*

friday
30

Kuumba (Creativity). *To do as much as we can, in whatever way we can, to leave our community more beautiful and beneficial than it was when we inherited it.*

saturday
31

JANUARY

s	m	t	w	t	f	s
1	2	3	4	5	6	7
8	9	10	11	12	13	14
15	16	17	18	19	20	21
22	23	24	25	26	27	28
29	30	31				

NEW YEAR'S DAY

Kwanzaa ends: Imani (Faith). *To believe with all our hearts in our people, our parents, our teachers, our leaders, and the righteousness and victory of our struggle.*

sunday
1

2011 INTERNATIONAL HOLIDAYS

Following are the dates of major holidays in 2011 for selected countries. Islamic observances are subject to adjustment. Holidays of the United States, the United Kingdom, and Canada, and major Jewish holidays, appear on this calendar's grid pages. Pomegranate is not responsible for errors or omissions in this list. All dates should be confirmed with local sources before making international travel or business plans. Please note: Most international holidays that fall on a weekend (or another holiday) are observed on the following Monday (or the next working day). This is not true, however, of Mexico, South Korea, or the Netherlands.

Argentina
- 1 Jan — New Year's Day
- 24 Mar — National Day of Memory for Truth and Justice
- 2 Apr — Veterans Day (Malvinas War Memorial)
- 21 Apr — Holy Thursday
- 22 Apr — Good Friday
- 24 Apr — Easter
- 1 May — Labor Day
- 25 May — Revolution Day
- 20 Jun — Flag Day*
- 9 Jul — Independence Day
- 15 Aug — San Martín Day*
- 12 Oct — Día de la Diversidad Cultural Americana†
- 8 Dec — Immaculate Conception
- 25 Dec — Christmas

* Observed on third Monday of month
† Observed on second Monday of October

Australia
- 1 Jan — New Year's Day
- 26 Jan — Australia Day
- 7 Mar — Labor Day (WA)
- 14 Mar — Labor Day (Vic)
  - Eight Hours Day (Tas)
  - Adelaide Cup (SA)
  - Canberra Day (ACT)
- 22–25 Apr — Easter Holiday
- 26 Apr — ANZAC Day
  - Easter Tuesday (Tas)
- 2 May — Labor Day (Qld)
  - May Day (NT)
- 6 Jun — Foundation Day (WA)
- 13 Jun — Queen's Birthday (except WA)
  - Volunteer's Day (SA)
- 1 Aug — Picnic Day (NT)
  - Bank Holiday (NSW)
- 3 Oct — Queen's Birthday (WA)
  - Labor Day (NSW, ACT, SA)
- 1 Nov — Melbourne Cup (Vic)
- 25 Dec — Christmas
- 26 Dec — Boxing Day (except SA)
  - Christmas Holiday (SA)
- 27 Dec — Proclamation Day (SA)

Brazil
- 1 Jan — New Year's Day
- 20 Jan — São Sebastião Day (Rio de Janeiro)
- 25 Jan — São Paulo Anniversary (São Paulo)
- 7–8 Mar — Carnival
- 9 Mar — Ash Wednesday (until 2 pm)
- 21 Apr — Tiradentes Day
- 22 Apr — Good Friday
- 24 Apr — Easter
- 1 May — Labor Day
- 23 Jun — Corpus Christi
- 7 Sep — Independence Day
- 12 Oct — Our Lady of Aparecida
- 2 Nov — All Souls' Day
- 15 Nov — Proclamation of the Republic
- 25 Dec — Christmas

China (see also Hong Kong)
- 1 Jan — New Year's Day
- 2 Feb — Chinese New Year Holiday begins
- 8 Feb — Last Day of New Year Holiday
- 5 Apr — Tomb-Sweeping Day
- 1 May — Labor Day
- 6 Jun — Dragon Boat Festival
- 12 Sep — Mid-Autumn Festival
- 26 Sep–2 Oct — National Day Holiday

France
- 1 Jan — New Year's Day
- 24 Apr — Easter
- 25 Apr — Easter Monday
- 1 May — Labor Day
- 8 May — Victory in Europe Day
- 2 Jun — Ascension Day
- 12 Jun — Pentecost
- 13 Jun — Whit Monday
- 14 Jul — Bastille Day
- 15 Aug — Assumption
- 1 Nov — All Saints' Day
- 11 Nov — Armistice Day
- 25 Dec — Christmas

Germany
- 1 Jan — New Year's Day
- 22 Apr — Good Friday
- 24 Apr — Easter
- 25 Apr — Easter Monday
- 1 May — Labor Day
- 2 Jun — Ascension Day
- 12 Jun — Pentecost
- 13 Jun — Whit Monday
- 3 Oct — Unity Day
- 25 Dec — Christmas
- 26 Dec — St. Stephen's Day

Hong Kong
- 1 Jan — New Year's Day
- 3–5 Feb — Spring Festival / Lunar New Year
- 2–5 Apr — Easter Holiday
- 5 Apr — Tomb-Sweeping Day
- 22 Apr — Good Friday
- 23 Apr — Holy Saturday
- 24 Apr — Easter
- 25 Apr — Easter Monday
- 1 May — Labor Day
- 10 May — Buddha's Birthday
- 6 Jun — Dragon Boat Festival
- 1 Jul — Special Administrative Region Establishment Day
- 13 Sep — Day After Mid-Autumn Festival
- 1 Oct — National Day
- 5 Oct — Chung Yeung Festival
- 25 Dec — Christmas
- 26 Dec — Boxing Day

India
- 1 Jan — New Year's Day
- 14 Jan — Makar Sankranti (North India)
- 15 Jan — Makar Sankranti (Bengal)
- 26 Jan — Republic Day
- 15 Feb — Prophet Muhammad's Birthday
- 16 Feb — Milad-un-Nabi
- 3 Mar — Maha Shivaratri
- 19 Mar — Holi
- 12 Apr — Ram Navami
- 14 Apr — Dr. B. R. Ambedkar's Birthday
- 16 Apr — Mahavir Jayanti
- 22 Apr — Good Friday
- 24 Apr — Easter
- 17 May — Buddha Purnima
- 15 Aug — Independence Day
- 21 Aug — Janamashtami
- 31 Aug — Ramzan-Eid (Eid al-Fitr)
- 2 Oct — Mahatma Gandhi's Birthday
- 26 Oct — Diwali (Deepavali)
- 7 Nov — Bakr-Eid (Eid al-Adha)
- 11 Nov — Guru Nanak's Birthday
- 6 Dec — Islamic New Year
- 25 Dec — Christmas

Ireland
- 1 Jan — New Year's Day
- 17 Mar — St. Patrick's Day
- 22 Apr — Good Friday
- 24 Apr — Easter
- 25 Apr — Easter Monday
- 2 May — Bank Holiday
- 6 Jun — Bank Holiday
- 1 Aug — Bank Holiday
- 31 Oct — Bank Holiday
- 25 Dec — Christmas
- 26 Dec — St. Stephen's Day

Israel
- 20 Mar — Purim (except Jerusalem)
- 21 Mar — Purim Bank Holiday (Jerusalem)
- 19 Apr — First Day of Pesach
- 25 Apr — Last Day of Pesach
- 1 May — Holocaust Memorial Day
- 9 May — National Memorial Day
- 10 May — Independence Day
- 8 Jun — Shavuot
- 9 Aug — Tisha B'Av
- 29–30 Sep — Rosh Hashanah
- 8 Oct — Yom Kippur
- 13 Oct — First Day of Sukkot
- 20 Oct — Shemini Atzeret / Simhat Torah

Italy
- 1 Jan — New Year's Day
- 6 Jan — Epiphany
- 24 Apr — Easter
- 25 Apr — Easter Monday
  - Liberation Day
- 1 May — Labor Day
- 2 Jun — Republic Day
- 29 Jun — Sts. Peter and Paul (Rome)

15	Aug	Assumption
1	Nov	All Saints' Day
8	Dec	Immaculate Conception
25	Dec	Christmas
26	Dec	St. Stephen's Day

JAPAN
1	Jan	New Year's Day
10	Jan	Coming of Age Day
11	Feb	National Foundation Day
21	Mar	Vernal Equinox
29	Apr	Shōwa Day
3	May	Constitution Memorial Day
4	May	Greenery Day
5	May	Children's Day
18	Jul	Marine Day
19	Sep	Respect for the Aged Day
23	Sep	Autumnal Equinox
10	Oct	Health and Sports Day
3	Nov	Culture Day
23	Nov	Labor Thanksgiving Day
23	Dec	Emperor's Birthday

MEXICO
1	Jan	New Year's Day
5	Feb	Constitution Day*
21	Mar	Benito Juárez Day†
21	Apr	Holy Thursday
22	Apr	Good Friday
24	Apr	Easter
1	May	Labor Day
16	Sep	Independence Day
1	Nov	All Saints' Day
2	Nov	All Souls' Day (Day of the Dead)
20	Nov	Revolution Day†
12	Dec	Our Lady of Guadalupe
25	Dec	Christmas

* Observed on first Monday of month
† Observed on third Monday of month

NETHERLANDS
1	Jan	New Year's Day
22	Apr	Good Friday
24	Apr	Easter
25	Apr	Easter Monday
30	Apr	Queen's Day
2	Jun	Ascension Day
12	Jun	Pentecost
13	Jun	Whit Monday
25-26	Dec	Christmas Holiday

NEW ZEALAND
1-2	Jan	New Year's Holiday
22	Jan	Provincial Anniversary (Wellington)*
29	Jan	Provincial Anniversary (Auckland)*
6	Feb	Waitangi Day
22	Apr	Good Friday
24	Apr	Easter
25	Apr	Easter Monday ANZAC Day
6	Jun	Queen's Birthday
24	Oct	Labor Day
11	Nov	Provincial Anniversary (Canterbury)
25	Dec	Christmas
26	Dec	Boxing Day

* Observed on closest Monday

PUERTO RICO
6	Jan	Three Kings Day (Epiphany)
11	Jan	Eugenio María de Hostos Day*
22	Mar	Emancipation Day
16	Apr	José de Diego Day†
22	Apr	Good Friday
24	Apr	Easter
17	Jul	Luis Muñoz Rivera Day†
25	Jul	Constitution Day
27	Jul	José Celso Barbosa Day
12	Oct	Día de la Raza*
19	Nov	Discovery of Puerto Rico
24	Dec	Christmas Eve

All US federal holidays also observed
* Observed on second Monday of month
† Observed on third Monday of month

RUSSIA
3	Jan	New Year's Holiday Begins
7	Jan	Orthodox Christmas
10	Jan	Last Day of New Year's Holiday
23	Feb	Defenders of the Fatherland Day
8	Mar	International Women's Day
24	Apr	Orthodox Easter
1	May	Spring and Labor Day
9	May	Victory Day
12	Jun	Independence Day
4	Nov	National Unity Day

SINGAPORE
1	Jan	New Year's Day
3-4	Feb	Chinese New Year Holiday
22	Apr	Good Friday
24	Apr	Easter
1	May	Labor Day
17	May	Vesak Day (Buddha's Birthday)
31	Jul	Beginning of Ramadan
9	Aug	National Day
29	Aug	Hari Raya Puasa (Eid al-Fitr)
26	Oct	Deepavali
5	Nov	Hari Raya Haji (Eid al-Adha)
25	Dec	Christmas

SOUTH AFRICA
1	Jan	New Year's Day
21	Mar	Human Rights Day
22	Apr	Good Friday
24	Apr	Easter
25	Apr	Family Day
27	Apr	Freedom Day
1	May	Workers' Day
16	Jun	Youth Day
9	Aug	National Women's Day
24	Sep	Heritage Day
16	Dec	Day of Reconciliation
25	Dec	Christmas
26	Dec	Day of Goodwill

SOUTH KOREA
1	Jan	New Year's Day
2-4	Feb	Lunar New Year Holiday
1	Mar	Independence Movement Day
5	May	Children's Day
10	May	Birth of Buddha
6	Jun	Memorial Day
17	Jul	Constitution Day
15	Aug	Independence Day
11-13	Sep	Harvest Moon Festival
3	Oct	National Foundation Day
25	Dec	Christmas

SPAIN
1	Jan	New Year's Day
6	Jan	Epiphany
21	Apr	Holy Thursday
22	Apr	Good Friday
24	Apr	Easter
1	May	Labor Day
15	Aug	Assumption
12	Oct	National Day
1	Nov	All Saints' Day
6	Dec	Constitution Day
8	Dec	Immaculate Conception
25	Dec	Christmas

SWEDEN
1	Jan	New Year's Day
5	Jan	Epiphany Eve
6	Jan	Epiphany
21	Apr	Maundy Thursday
22	Apr	Good Friday
24	Apr	Easter
25	Apr	Easter Monday
30	Apr	Walpurgis Eve King's Birthday
1	May	May Day
1	Jun	Day Before Ascension
2	Jun	Ascension Day
6	Jun	National Day
12	Jun	Pentecost
24	Jun	Midsummer Eve
25	Jun	Midsummer Day
4	Nov	All Saints' Eve
5	Nov	All Saints' Day
24	Dec	Christmas Eve
25	Dec	Christmas
26	Dec	Boxing Day
31	Dec	New Year's Eve

SWITZERLAND
1	Jan	New Year's Day
22	Apr	Good Friday
24	Apr	Easter
25	Apr	Easter Monday
2	Jun	Ascension Day
12	Jun	Pentecost
13	Jun	Whit Monday
1	Aug	National Day
25	Dec	Christmas

THAILAND
1	Jan	New Year's Day
18	Feb	Makha Bucha Day
6	Apr	Chakri Day
13-15	Apr	Songkran (Thai New Year)
1	May	Labor Day
5	May	Coronation Day
17	May	Visakha Bucha Day (Buddha's Birthday)
15	Jul	Asanha Bucha Day
16	Jul	Khao Phansa (Buddhist Lent begins)
12	Aug	Queen's Birthday
23	Oct	Chulalongkorn Day
10	Nov	Loy Kratong
5	Dec	King's Birthday
10	Dec	Constitution Day
31	Dec	New Year's Eve

WORLD TIME ZONE MAP

This map is based on Coordinated Universal Time (UTC), the worldwide system of civil timekeeping. UTC is essentially equivalent to Greenwich Mean Time. Zone boundaries are approximate and subject to change. Time differences relative to UTC shown here are based on the use of standard time; where Daylight Saving Time (Summer Time) is employed, add one hour to local standard time.

Svalbard (NORWAY)
FRANZ JOSEF LAND
SEVERNAYA ZEMLYA
ARCTIC OCEAN
NEW SIBERIAN ISLANDS
Kara Sea
Laptev Sea
East Siberian Sea
Barents Sea
NOVAYA ZEMLYA
Norwegian Sea
Chukchi Sea
Bering Sea
NORWAY
SWEDEN
FINLAND
RUSSIA
North Sea
UNITED KINGDOM
POLAND
GERMANY
BELARUS
UKRAINE
FRANCE
ITALY
ROMANIA
BULGARIA
GREECE
TURKEY
Black Sea
Caspian Sea
GEORGIA
ARMENIA
AZERBAIJAN
KAZAKHSTAN
UZBEKISTAN
KYRGYZSTAN
TAJIKISTAN
MONGOLIA
CHINA
NORTH KOREA
SOUTH KOREA
JAPAN
Sea of Japan
Sea of Okhotsk
KURIL ISLANDS
ALEUTIAN ISLANDS
NORTH PACIFIC OCEAN
International Date Line
Eastward across Date Line
Subtract 24 hours
Westward across Date Line
Add 24 hours
MALTA
TUNISIA
CYPRUS
SYRIA
LEBANON
ISRAEL
JORDAN
IRAQ
IRAN
KUWAIT
Persian Gulf
QATAR
AFGHANISTAN
PAKISTAN
Mediterranean Sea
ALGERIA
LIBYA
EGYPT
SAUDI ARABIA
OMAN
YEMEN
Red Sea
Arabian Sea
INDIA
NEPAL
BHUTAN
BANGLADESH
BURMA
LAOS
THAILAND
VIETNAM
CAMBODIA
Bay of Bengal
South China Sea
Philippine Sea
PHILIPPINES
Ryukyu Islands (JAPAN)
Northern Mariana Islands (U.S.)
Guam (U.S.)
FEDERATED STATES OF MICRONESIA
MARSHALL ISLANDS
PALAU
NAURU
KIRIBATI
SRI LANKA
MALDIVES
Andaman Islands (INDIA)
Nicobar Islands (INDIA)
MALAYSIA
SINGAPORE
INDONESIA
TIMOR LESTE
PAPUA NEW GUINEA
SOLOMON ISLANDS
TUVALU
SAMOA
VANUATU
FIJI
Coral Islands (AUSTL.)
SUDAN
CHAD
NIGER
NIGERIA
BURKINA FASO
TOGO
GHANA
BENIN
CAMEROON
CENTRAL AFRICAN REPUBLIC
EQUATORIAL GUINEA
SÃO TOMÉ AND PRÍNCIPE
GABON
REP. OF THE CONGO
DEM. REP. OF THE CONGO
ERITREA
DJIBOUTI
ETHIOPIA
SOMALIA
UGANDA
KENYA
RWANDA
BURUNDI
TANZANIA
SEYCHELLES
COMOROS
ANGOLA
ZAMBIA
MALAWI
MOZAMBIQUE
ZIMBABWE
NAMIBIA
BOTSWANA
MADAGASCAR
MAURITIUS
SOUTH AFRICA
SWAZILAND
LESOTHO
St. Helena (U.K.)
INDIAN OCEAN
AUSTRALIA
TASMANIA
NEW ZEALAND
Prince Edward Islands (SOUTH AFRICA)
ÎLES CROZET
French Southern and Antarctic Lands (FRANCE)
0
+1
+2
+3
+4
+5
+6
+7
+8
+9
+10
+11
+12

2012

JANUARY

s	m	t	w	t	f	s
1	2	3	4	5	6	7
8	9	10	11	12	13	14
15	16	17	18	19	20	21
22	23	24	25	26	27	28
29	30	31				

FEBRUARY

s	m	t	w	t	f	s
			1	2	3	4
5	6	7	8	9	10	11
12	13	14	15	16	17	18
19	20	21	22	23	24	25
26	27	28	29			

MARCH

s	m	t	w	t	f	s
				1	2	3
4	5	6	7	8	9	10
11	12	13	14	15	16	17
18	19	20	21	22	23	24
25	26	27	28	29	30	31

APRIL

s	m	t	w	t	f	s
1	2	3	4	5	6	7
8	9	10	11	12	13	14
15	16	17	18	19	20	21
22	23	24	25	26	27	28
29	30					

MAY

s	m	t	w	t	f	s
		1	2	3	4	5
6	7	8	9	10	11	12
13	14	15	16	17	18	19
20	21	22	23	24	25	26
27	28	29	30	31		

JUNE

s	m	t	w	t	f	s
					1	2
3	4	5	6	7	8	9
10	11	12	13	14	15	16
17	18	19	20	21	22	23
24	25	26	27	28	29	30

2012

JULY

s	m	t	w	t	f	s
1	2	3	4	5	6	7
8	9	10	11	12	13	14
15	16	17	18	19	20	21
22	23	24	25	26	27	28
29	30	31				

AUGUST

s	m	t	w	t	f	s
			1	2	3	4
5	6	7	8	9	10	11
12	13	14	15	16	17	18
19	20	21	22	23	24	25
26	27	28	29	30	31	

SEPTEMBER

s	m	t	w	t	f	s
						1
2	3	4	5	6	7	8
9	10	11	12	13	14	15
16	17	18	19	20	21	22
23	24	25	26	27	28	29
30						

OCTOBER

s	m	t	w	t	f	s
	1	2	3	4	5	6
7	8	9	10	11	12	13
14	15	16	17	18	19	20
21	22	23	24	25	26	27
28	29	30	31			

NOVEMBER

s	m	t	w	t	f	s
				1	2	3
4	5	6	7	8	9	10
11	12	13	14	15	16	17
18	19	20	21	22	23	24
25	26	27	28	29	30	

DECEMBER

s	m	t	w	t	f	s
						1
2	3	4	5	6	7	8
9	10	11	12	13	14	15
16	17	18	19	20	21	22
23	24	25	26	27	28	29
30	31					

Notes

Notes

Personal Information

name _____

address _____

city _____ *state* _____ *zip* _____

phone _____

cell/pgr _____ *fax* _____

e-mail _____

in case of emergency, please notify:

name _____

address _____

city _____ *state* _____ *zip* _____

phone _____

physician's name _____

physician's phone _____

health insurance company _____

plan number _____

allergies _____

other _____

driver's license number _____

car insurance company _____

policy number _____